First World War

and Army of Occupation

War Diary

France, Belgium and Germany

39 DIVISION
Divisional Troops
Machine Gun Corps
39 Battalion
1 March 1918 - 19 March 1918

WO95/2577/4

The Naval & Military Press Ltd
www.nmarchive.com
Published in association with The National Archives

Published by

The Naval & Military Press Ltd

Unit 10 Ridgewood Industrial Park,

Uckfield, East Sussex,

TN22 5QE England

Tel: +44 (0) 1825 749494

www.naval-military-press.com

www.nmarchive.com

This diary has been reprinted in facsimile from the original. Any imperfections are inevitably reproduced and the quality may fall short of modern type and cartographic standards.

Contents

Document type	Place/Title	Date From	Date To
Heading	WO95/2577/4		
Heading	39 Div Troops 39 Bn MG Corps 1918 Mar To 1919 Mar		
Heading	39th Battalion Machine Gun Corps. March 1918		
Heading	War Diary 39th Battalion Machine Gun Corps Lt. Col A. Fleet Wood Wilson		
War Diary			
War Diary	Ref Maps Villers-Guslain Gauche Wood 57c S.E	01/03/1918	11/03/1918
War Diary	Haut Allaines	11/03/1918	21/03/1918
War Diary	Gurlu Wood Ref Map 1/20,000 62 C N.E	22/03/1918	22/03/1918
War Diary	Frise Map 1/40000 62c	23/03/1918	23/03/1918
War Diary	Frise	24/03/1918	25/03/1918
War Diary	Ref. Map 1/10,000 62D S.E.	25/03/1918	25/03/1918
War Diary	Proyart	26/03/1918	26/03/1918
War Diary	Hamel	27/03/1918	27/03/1918
War Diary	Domart Sur La Luce Ref. Map 62 D Font Ed	28/03/1918	28/03/1918
War Diary	Domart Sur La Luce	29/03/1918	29/03/1918
War Diary	Boves Ref Map Amiens 1/100000	30/03/1918	30/03/1918
War Diary	Bovelles	31/03/1918	31/03/1918
Heading	39th Battalion Machine Gun Corps April 1918		
Miscellaneous	D.A.G., 3rd Echelon.	01/05/1918	01/05/1918
Heading	War Diary of 39 Bn. Machine Gun Corps From 1st April to 30th April 1918 (Volume II)		
War Diary	Ref Amiens 17 1/100000 Bovelles	01/04/1918	01/04/1918
War Diary	Ref Dieppe 1/100000	02/04/1918	03/04/1918
War Diary	Villeroy	04/04/1918	10/04/1918
War Diary	Ref Sheet France 36 A	10/04/1918	11/04/1918
War Diary	Ref Sheet France 36A 1/40000	11/04/1918	11/04/1918
War Diary	Ref France 36 A 1/40000	12/04/1918	13/04/1918
War Diary	Hamen Artois	14/04/1918	17/04/1918
War Diary	Ref France 36A 1/40000 Ham En Artois	13/04/1918	30/04/1918
Heading	39th Battalion Machine Gun Corps. May 1918		
Heading	War Diary Of 39th Bn. Machine Gun Corps From May 1st To May 31st 1918 Volume III		
War Diary	Ref.map France 36 A 1/40000 Ham En Artois	01/05/1918	22/05/1918
War Diary	Ref. Map France 36A 1/40000 Rombly	23/05/1918	31/05/1918
Heading	War Diary Of 39th Battalion Machine Gun Corps. June 1st 1918 to June 30th 1918 Volume IV		
War Diary	Ref. Sheet France 36A 1/40000 Rombly	01/06/1918	15/06/1918
War Diary	Ref Sheet France 36a 1/10000 La Pecqueur 12O C	15/06/1918	15/06/1918
War Diary	Rombly	16/06/1918	16/06/1918
War Diary	La Pecqueur	16/06/1918	16/06/1918
War Diary	Rombly	17/06/1918	17/06/1918
War Diary	La Pecqueur	17/06/1918	17/06/1918
War Diary	Rombly	18/06/1918	18/06/1918
War Diary	Ref Sheet France 36 A 1/40,000 Rombly 18b. La Pecqueur	18/06/1918	18/06/1918
War Diary	Rombly La Pecqueur Rombly	19/06/1918	24/06/1918
War Diary	La Pecqueur	25/06/1918	25/06/1918
War Diary	Ref Sheet France 36 A 1/40,000 La Pecqueur Rombly	25/06/1918	26/06/1918

War Diary	La Pecqueur	26/06/1918	26/06/1918
War Diary	Ref Sheet France 36 A 1/40,000 Rombly La Pecqueur	27/06/1918	28/06/1918
War Diary	Ref Sheet France 36A 1/40,000 R9,14	28/06/1918	28/06/1918
War Diary	Rombly K9. 14	29/06/1918	30/06/1918
Miscellaneous	War Diary Of 39th (Army) Machine Gun Battalion		
War Diary	Ref Sheet France 36a 1/40,000 Rombly K 9.14	01/07/1918	01/07/1918
War Diary	Rombly La Pecqueur Rombly	02/07/1918	09/07/1918
War Diary	Ref Sheet France 36A 1/40,000 Rombly	10/07/1918	26/07/1918
War Diary	H 7 C.d	27/07/1918	31/07/1918
War Diary	Ref France Sheet 36a 1/40,000 Rombly	01/08/1918	18/08/1918
War Diary	Ref Sheet Hazebrouck 5A 1/100,000		
War Diary	Ref Sheet France 36A 1/40,000 Rombly	19/08/1918	26/08/1918
War Diary	Ref Hazebrouck 5a 1/100,000 And Lens II 1/100,000 Rombly	27/08/1918	27/08/1918
War Diary	Houdain		
War Diary	Ref France Lens II 1/100,000 Houdain	28/08/1918	28/08/1918
War Diary	Ref 51B 1/40,000 Arras	29/08/1918	29/08/1918
War Diary	Ref Sheet France 51 B 1/40,000 H 34d 2.9	29/08/1918	29/08/1918
War Diary	Ref Sheet France 51B 1/40,000 O7b6.3	29/08/1918	30/08/1918
War Diary	Ref. Sheet France 51B 1/40,000	30/08/1918	30/08/1918
War Diary	O8 C 2.7		
War Diary	Ref. Sheet France 51B 1/40,000	30/08/1918	30/08/1918
War Diary	Vicinity of Boiry Notre Dame	31/08/1918	31/08/1918
War Diary	Ref Sheet France 51B 1/40,000	31/08/1918	31/08/1918
Heading	39th (Army) Machine Gun Battalion War Diary From 1st Sept To 30th Sept 1918 Volume VII		
War Diary	Ref France Sheet 51 B 1/40,000 Bn H.Q. O 8 C 2.9.	01/09/1918	05/09/1918
War Diary	Ref France Sheet 51B 1/40,000 Bn H.Q. O8c2.9 Bn H.Q. G30d0.4	06/09/1918	08/09/1918
War Diary	Ref France Sheet 51 B 1/40,000	08/09/1918	08/09/1918
War Diary	G 30d 0. 4 Lens II 1/100,000	09/09/1918	09/09/1918
War Diary	Gauchin-Le Gal (H2.00.95) Hazebrouck 5a 1/100,000 Lieres (F 6.65.60	10/09/1918	10/09/1918
War Diary	Ref France Sheet Hazebrouck 5A 1/100,000 Lieres Morbecque 36A NE 36NW 1/20,000	11/09/1918	15/09/1918
War Diary	Ref France 36A NE 36NW Morbecque F24a 2.7	15/09/1918	16/09/1918
War Diary	Ref France Sheet 36NW 36A NE) 1/20,000	16/09/1918	18/09/1918
Miscellaneous			
War Diary	Ref France Sheet 36 NW 36A NE 1/40,000 F24a 10.75	19/09/1918	22/09/1918
Miscellaneous			
War Diary	Ref France Sheet 36 NW 36A NE 1/20,000 Bn. H.Q. F24a 10.75	22/09/1918	24/09/1918
Miscellaneous			
War Diary	Ref France Sheet 36 NE 1/20,000 Bn H.Q. F24a 10.75	24/09/1918	27/09/1918
Miscellaneous			
War Diary	France Sheet 36N.W. 36A NE 1/20,000 Bn. H.Q. F.24.O.10.75	28/09/1918	30/09/1918
Miscellaneous			
Heading	War Diary Of 39th (Army) Machine Gun Battalion. From 1st October 1918 To 31st October 1918 Volume VIII		
Miscellaneous			
War Diary	France Sheet 36 N.W. 36A NE Bah. H.Q. F.24.a.10.75	01/10/1918	02/10/1918
Miscellaneous			
War Diary	France Sheets 36NW 36A.NE Battn. H.Q F.24.A.10.75	02/10/1918	02/10/1918
Miscellaneous			

War Diary	France Sheet 36 N.W. 36. A.NE Batt H.Q. F.24. A.10.75	02/10/1918	02/10/1918
War Diary	Battn HQ. F.24.A. 10.75 to A. 23.B.1.9	03/10/1918	03/10/1918
Miscellaneous			
War Diary	France Sheet 36 N.W. 36.A. N. E Batt HQ. A.23.B.1.9	03/10/1918	03/10/1918
Miscellaneous			
War Diary	France Sheet 36 N.W. 36.A. NE Batt H.Q. A. 23.B.1.9	04/10/1918	05/10/1918
Miscellaneous			
War Diary	France 36 N. W 36 A. NE Batt. H.Q. A.23.B.19	04/10/1918	05/10/1918
Miscellaneous			
War Diary	France 36 N.W. 36A N E Batt. H.Q.A. 23. B.1.9	05/10/1918	06/10/1918
Miscellaneous			
War Diary	France 36. N.W. 36 A.N.E Batt H.Q. A.23.B.1.9	07/10/1918	08/10/1918
Miscellaneous			
War Diary	France 36 N.W. 36.A. NE. Batt H.Q. A.23. B.1.9	09/10/1918	12/10/1918
Miscellaneous			
War Diary	France Sheet 36 NW 36.A N E Batt HQ. F.24.a10.75	13/10/1918	14/10/1918
Miscellaneous			
War Diary	France Sheet 36 N.W. 36A N E Batt H.Q. F.24a.10.75	15/10/1918	18/10/1918
Miscellaneous			
War Diary	France Sheet 36 Batt H.Q. B. 30c 92	18/10/1918	19/10/1918
War Diary	Batt H.Q E26 C 81.15	20/10/1918	22/10/1918
Miscellaneous			
War Diary	France Sheet 36 Batt H.Q. E 26.c 8115	24/10/1918	24/10/1918
War Diary	Sheet 37 Batt HQ S6d 42	25/10/1918	26/10/1918
Miscellaneous			
War Diary	France Sheet 37 Batt H.Q G6d 42	27/10/1918	28/10/1918
Miscellaneous			
War Diary	France Sheet 37 Batt H.Q. G 6d 42	29/10/1918	31/10/1918
Miscellaneous			
Heading	War Diary Of 39th (Army) Machine Gun Battalion.Volume 10		
Miscellaneous			
War Diary	France Sheet 37 Battn HQ G6d 4.2	01/12/1918	04/12/1918
Miscellaneous			
War Diary		05/12/1918	07/12/1918
Miscellaneous			
War Diary		08/12/1918	11/12/1918
Miscellaneous			
War Diary		12/12/1918	16/12/1918
Miscellaneous			
War Diary		17/12/1918	21/12/1918
Miscellaneous			
War Diary		22/12/1918	27/12/1918
Miscellaneous			
War Diary		26/12/1918	31/12/1918
Miscellaneous			
Heading	War Diary 39th (Army) Machine Gun Battalion From 1st January 1919 To January 31st 1919 Volume II		
War Diary			
War Diary	France Sheet 37 Battn M.G.C. b d 42	01/01/1919	11/01/1919
Miscellaneous			
War Diary	France Sheet 37 Battn M.G.c6d 42	12/01/1919	21/01/1919
Miscellaneous			
War Diary	France Sheet 37 Batn M.G.C. 6d 42	22/01/1919	31/01/1919
Miscellaneous			

Heading	War Diary Of 39th (Army) Machine Gun Battalion From 1st February 1919 To 28 February 1919 Volume 12		
Miscellaneous			
War Diary	France Sheet 37 Battn M.G. G.b.d 42	01/02/1919	08/02/1919
Miscellaneous			
War Diary		09/02/1919	20/02/1919
Miscellaneous			
War Diary		21/02/1919	28/02/1919
Miscellaneous			
Heading	War Diary Of 39th (Army) Machine Gun Battalion From 1st March 1919 To 19th March 1919		
War Diary			
War Diary	France Sheet 37G bd 4020 M.G. Batt	01/03/1919	13/03/1919
Miscellaneous			
War Diary	Sheet 3612 9b64	14/03/1918	19/03/1918
Miscellaneous			
Heading	2 Div		
Miscellaneous			

WO95/2577/4

39 DIV TROOPS

39 BN MG
CORPS

1918 MAR
TO
1919 MAR

39th Div.

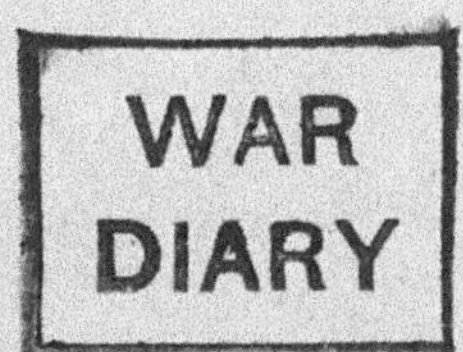

39th BATTALION, MACHINE GUN CORPS.

M A R C H

1 9 1 8

FOLIO I

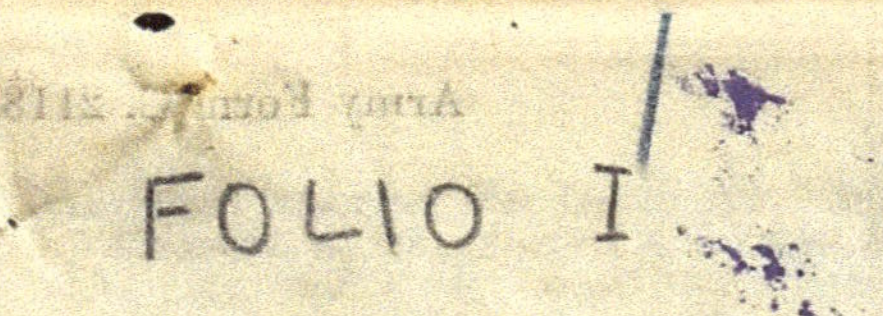

MARCH 1918

Vol 1

WAR DIARY

39th Battalion, Machine Gun Corps

Lt. Col. A. Fleetwood Wilson
Comdg.

Instructions regarding War Diaries and Intelligence Summaries are contained in F. S. Regs., Part II. and the Staff Manual respectively. Title pages will be prepared in manuscript.

WAR DIARY
or
~~INTELLIGENCE SUMMARY.~~
(Erase heading not required.)

Army Form C. 2118.

Place	Date	Hour	Summary of Events and Information	Remarks and references to Appendices
			This is the first War Diary compiled by the 39th Bn. M. G. Corps. Coys. referred to as 'A', 'B', 'C' & 'D' were respectively 116th, 117th, 118th & 228th M.G. Coys.	A.H.J.

D. D. & L., London, E.C.
(A8204) Wt W1771/M2031 750,000 5/17 Sch. 52 Forms/C2118/14

Army Form C. 2118.

Instructions regarding War Diaries and Intelligence Summaries are contained in F. S. Regs., Part II. and the Staff Manual respectively. Title pages will be prepared in manuscript.

WAR DIARY
or
~~INTELLIGENCE SUMMARY.~~

(Erase heading not required.)

Place	Date	Hour	Summary of Events and Information	Remarks and references to Appendices
Ref. maps VILLERS-GUSLAIN GAUCHE WOOD 57C S.E.	1.3.18.		'B' Coy. relieved by 64th M.G. Coy. Relief complete 11.30 p.m. Went to HEUDICOURT. 'A' Coy. 3 sections in line, 1 section in reserve at HEUDICOURT 'C' Coy 3 sections in line " " " " " 'D' Coy " " " " " " " " "	A.H.S.
	2.3.18.		'B' Coy, 2 sections relieved 1 section each of 197th and 'D' Coys. in GOUZEAUCOURT SECTOR 'A' Coy, as for 1.3.18. 6,000 rds fired on S.O.S. lines. Nos. 6 and 7 positions relieved by 62nd M.G. Coy. and were transferred to W.6.c.45.45 & W.6.c.35.95 Harassing Fire 1700 rds. fired.	A.H.S.
	3.3.18.		Coys. formed into battalion under Lt. Col. A. Fleetwood Wilson 4th Q.O.H. for Tactical Purposes, still under Bdes. for Administration.	A.H.S.
	4.3.18.		Trench Routine. Gun positions for defence of HEUDICOURT allotted by Town Major.	A.H.S.
	5.3.18.		Trench Routine. Harassing Fire 1250 rds.	A.H.S.
	6.3.18.	4.30 a.m.	S.O.S. on Right Bde. Front. 28 000 rds. Fired.	Wounded one O.R. A.H.S.
	7.3.18.		Trench Routine. Usual harassing fire on tracks and M.G. Emplacements.	A.H.S.
	8.3.18.		" " " " " " " " "	A.H.S.

D. D. & L., London, E.C. (A8204) Wt W1771/M2031 750,000 5/17 Sch. 52 Forms/C2118/14

Army Form C. 2118.

WAR DIARY
or
~~INTELLIGENCE~~ SUMMARY.

(*Erase heading not required.*)

Instructions regarding War Diaries and Intelligence Summaries are contained in F. S. Regs., Part II. and the Staff Manual respectively. Title pages will be prepared in manuscript.

Place	Date	Hour	Summary of Events and Information	Remarks and references to Appendices
	9.3.18.		Trench Routine. 5000 rds. in cooperation with infantry raids.	H.H.S
	10.3.18		Trench Routine. S.O.S. answered on Left Bde. Front. Harassing fire at night.	H.H.S
HAUT	11.3.18. to 13.3.18.		Coys. were relieved in turn in the line by 9th M.G. Battn. and proceeded by rail to HAUT ALLAINES	H.H.S.
ALLAINES	14.3.18. to 20.3.18		Completion of amalgamation of Coys. into a battalion. Training and refitting.	18th Wounded Capt. WHITBY H.H.S.

D. D. & L., London, E.C. (A8004) Wt W1771/M2031 750,000 5/17 Sch. 52 Forms/C2116/14

Army Form C. 2118.

Instructions regarding War Diaries and Intelligence Summaries are contained in F. S. Regs., Part II. and the Staff Manual respectively. Title pages will be prepared in manuscript.

WAR DIARY
or
~~INTELLIGENCE SUMMARY.~~
(Erase heading not required.)

Place	Date	Hour	Summary of Events and Information	Remarks and references to Appendices
HAUT ALLAINES	21.3.18	5.50 am	'A', 'B', and 'C' Coys were ordered to move to Concentration Point near NURLU, and were attached to 116, 117, and 118 Inf. Bdes. respectively. Bn. HQ and 'D' Coy. to remain at HAUT ALLAINES	
		8.30 am	Move complete	
		4 p.m.	'B' Coy with 116 Inf. Bde: was attached to 16th Div: and moved to St EMILIE, one section attached to 1/1st Herts Regt, and 1 Section to 13th Royal Sussex Regt., the remaining two sections at L.18.d.2.9., left Bde. HQ of 16th Div:	
		8.15 p.m	'A' Coy. moved to BROWN LINE near SAULCOURT to dig emplacements 'C' Coy. with HQ at LONGAVESNES occupied 118 Bde. portion of the SAULCOURT—TINCOURT WOOD SWITCH LINE. At night our troops were holding EPÉHY and ST. EMILIE. Battalion HQ moved to GURLU WOOD together with 'D' Coy.	H.H.S.
GURLU WOOD Ref. Map 1/20000 62C N.E.	22.3.18	10.30 am	'A' Coy. HQ moved to LONGAVESNES, guns all intact and occupying left Bde. Section of SAULCOURT – TINCOURT WOOD SWITCH LINE 'B' Coy. HQ moved to LONGAVESNES, guns fighting rearguard action with infantry to which they were attached 'C' Coy. HQ still at LONGAVESNES, guns occupying TINCOURT WOOD – SAULCOURT SWITCH 'D' Coy. One section sent to defend GREEN LINE South of TINCOURT WOOD, one section to cover north edge of wood, and to cover any retirement from the SWITCH LINE upon it. Two sections ~~attached~~ sent to cover 118 Bde. front. In the dark 117 and 118 Inf. Bdes. retired to the GREEN LINE, 116 Bde. being still attd to 16th Div: Battn. HQ returned to HAUT ALLAINES. In case of a further retirement positions were reconnoitred for three companies East of BUSSU. On this day the enemy reached HAMEL.	Casualties Officers. K. 1, W. 3, M. 1 O.R's. K. 4, W. 19, M. 24 2/Lt. G.E. HALE K. T/2/Lt. MOODIE W. ~~[illegible]~~ Lt. G.R. OATES W. 2/Lt. E.P. GOULDING W. 2/Lt. R.J. PRITCHARD M. H.H.S.

D. D & L., London, E.C. (A8204) Wt W1771/M2031 750,000 5/17 Sch. 52 Forms/C2118/14

Instructions regarding War Diaries and Intelligence Summaries are contained in F. S. Regs., Part II. and the Staff Manual respectively. Title pages will be prepared in manuscript.

WAR DIARY
or
~~INTELLIGENCE SUMMARY.~~

(Erase heading not required.)

Army Form C. 2118.

Place	Date	Hour	Summary of Events and Information	Remarks and references to Appendices
FRISE Map. 1/40000 62C	23.3.18		The enemy advance being too rapid for successful resistance on the line East of BUSSU, the Division retired to CLERY, 118 Inf. Bde. with 'B' Coy. being detailed to hold LA MAISONNETTE, and 116 Inf. Bde. the spur in B.29 and B23, with 117 Inf. Bde. at FEUILLERES. Divnl. HQ moved from HAUT ALLAINES to CLERY and thence to FRISE. Battn. HQ, Transport and 'A' Coy. moved to a point a few hundred yards west of HERBECOURT. 'D' Coy. on arrival at CLERY was ordered to defend the line taken up by 116 and 118 Inf. Bdes. Six guns got scattered and lost, two of them being destroyed, by shell-fire on the road. On moving up to take up the positions, which had been previously reconnoitred, the guns which were to be on the right bank of the SOMME RIVER, were prevented from crossing the river by the impending demolition of the bridge. They were therefore kept at FEUILLERES. At night 'D' Coy. took over the task allotted to 'B' Coy., of which, of the remaining eight guns, six returned to the Transport Line, and two remained in action. 'C' Coy. had nine guns in action. 8 guns of 16th Div. were attached to the Battn for action.	Casualties Officers K. | W. | M. – | – | 3 O.R's. K. | W. | M 1 | 3 | – 2/Lt. W.A. NEWMAN. M. Lt. H.A. CUTLER. M. Lt. A.S. TIGHT. M. H.H.S.
FRISE	24.3.18		Battn. HQ, Transport, and Details moved west along HERBECOURT–CAPPY ROAD, and were parked about ¼ mile west of CAPPY.	Casualties O.R's. K. | W. | M. 0 | 6 | 2 H.H.S.
		5 p.m.	'A' Coy. was ordered to relieve 'C' Coy. in the line with twelve guns. Divnl. HQ. moved to CHUIGNES.	
FRISE	25.3.18		'A' Coy relieved 'C' Coy in line; eight guns in forward positions, 4 in reserve at HERBECOURT. Relief complete 6.30. a.m.	Casualties O.R's. K | W. | M 2 | 6 | 1 H.H.S.
		12 noon	4 Res. guns of 'A' Coy. moved off to report to O.C. 6th Bn. Cheshire Regt. for action. 'D' Coy. had 4 guns with 117 Bde., four guns with 118 Bde, two guns in reserve at G.31. a.5.0. All guns in action withdrew by order with infantry to HERBECOURT–FRISE LINE Bn. HQ., Transport, and Details withdrew to huts 1½ miles South of CAPPY.	

D. D. & L., London, E.C. (A8204) Wt W1771/M2031 750,000 5/17 Sch. 52 Forms/C2118/14

Army Form C. 2118.

WAR DIARY
or
~~INTELLIGENCE~~ SUMMARY.

(*Erase heading not required.*)

Instructions regarding War Diaries and Intelligence Summaries are contained in F. S. Regs., Part II. and the Staff Manual respectively. Title pages will be prepared in manuscript.

Place	Date	Hour	Summary of Events and Information	Remarks and references to Appendices
Ref. Map 1/10,000 62D S.E.	25.3.18 (cont.)		~~Divnl. HQ moved to PROYART~~ Divnl. HQ moved to CHUIGNES 'A' Coy: on occupation of FRISE–HERBECOURT LINE had twelve guns with 118 Bde; 'D' Coy 4 guns with 118 Bde., and Six guns with 117 Bde	H. H. S.
PROYART	~~26.3.18~~ 26.3.18.	1 p.m.	Divnl. HQ moved to PROYART 'B' Coy: with 10 guns under G.O.C. 117 and 118 Inf. Bdes. moved to PROYART – FRAMERVILLE LINE. 'C' Coy with 10 guns was attached to 116 Inf Bde in reserve at about Q.30. Divnl. HQ moved to HAMEL 'A' Coy and 'D' Coy were withdrawn and billetted in VAIRE SOUS CORBIE.	Casualties O.R's. K. – W. 3 M. 9 H. H. S.
HAMEL	27.3.18.		The fact that the enemy thrust forward to SAILLY LESEC caused Transport and Details to move to BOIS DE VAIRE	
		7.40 a.m.	Our line ran X.2.b.1.5., R.32.d.4.0. R.32.d.1.9., R.33.a. central One complete section of 4 guns was sent to report to G.O.C. 116 Inf Bde. ~~in~~ Q.30.c. A composite company of 14 guns took up positions in the valley East of HAMEL Divnl. HQ. moved first to HAMELET and then to FOUILLOY. Battn. HQ, Transport and Details moved to vicinity of HAMELET.	Casualties Officers. K. – W. 2 M. – O.R's. K. – W. 13 M. 4 H. H. S. T/Capt. EILERINGTON. W T/Lt. C.J. CRAWLEY. W.
DOMART SUR LA LUCE Ref. Map 62 D First. Ed.	28.3.18.		Divnl. HQ moved to DOMART SUR LA LUCE, also Bn. HQ, Transport and Details. The composite Coy., now numbering 12 guns, were withdrawn from HAMEL – WARFUSÉE LINE and sent to IGNAUCOURT to take over MARCELCAVE – WIENCOURT line from 'B' Coy. Four of these guns manned the line, and the remainder returned to Details at DOMART SUR LA LUCE A further four guns were attached to 117 Inf. Bde. - Units of 116 Inf Bde. were attached to 118 Inf. Bde. for Tactical Purposes.	Casualties O.R's. K. 1 W. 2 M. – H. H. S.
DOMART SUR LA LUCE	29.3.18.	6 a.m.	Six guns were were sent to take up positions in U.15. central to cover any retirement from MARCELCAVE – IGNAUCOURT LINE. Divnl. HQ. Bn. HQ. Transport and Details moved to BOVES.	H. H. S.

D. D. & L., London, E.C. (A8004) Wt W1771/M2031 750,000 5/17 Sch. 52 Forms/C2118/14

Army Form C. 2118.

Instructions regarding War Diaries and Intelligence Summaries are contained in F. S. Regs., Part II. and the Staff Manual respectively. Title pages will be prepared in manuscript.

WAR DIARY
or
~~INTELLIGENCE SUMMARY.~~
(Erase heading not required.)

Place	Date	Hour	Summary of Events and Information	Remarks and references to Appendices
BOVES Ref. Map. AMIENS 1/100000	30.3.18		Divnl. HQ, Bn. HQ, Transport and Details at BOVES. at night Division was withdrawn from the line. men coming out of the line were met, fed, and billetted near LONGEAU.	H.H.
BOVELLES	31.3.18		The battalion moved to BOVELLES.	H.H.

[signature] Lt Col.
Commanding 39th Battn Machine Gun Corps

D. D. & L., London, E.C.
(A8004) Wt W1771/M2031 750,000 5/17 Sch. 52 Forms/C2118/14

39th Divisional Troops

39th BATTALION

MACHINE GUN CORPS

APRIL 1918.

8

D.A.G.,

3rd. Echelon.

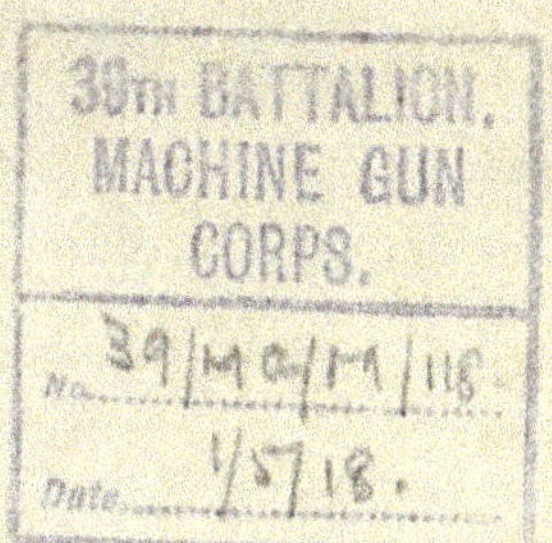
39TH BATTALION,
MACHINE GUN
CORPS.
No. 39/MG/M/118
Date 1/5/18.

Enclosed please find War Diary for this unit for April, 1918.

[signature]

Lieut.Col.,

1st.May,1918 — Comdg. 39th.Bn.Machine Gun Corps.

39

Vol 2

CONFIDENTIAL

War Diary
of
39 Bn. Machine Gun Corps

from 1st April to 30th April 1918

(Volume II.)

Army Form C. 2118.

Instructions regarding War Diaries and Intelligence Summaries are contained in F. S. Regs., Part II. and the Staff Manual respectively. Title pages will be prepared in manuscript.

WAR DIARY
or
~~INTELLIGENCE SUMMARY.~~
(Erase heading not required.)

Place	Date	Hour	Summary of Events and Information	Remarks and references to Appendices
Ref. AMIENS 17 1/100 000				
BOVELLES	1.4.18		Resting and cleaning up. Three officers and their gun detachments reported from LONGEAU	H.H.S.
Ref. DIEPPE 1/100,000	2.4.18		The battalion moved by march route to WARLUS	H.H.S.
	3.4.18		The battalion moved by march route to VILLEROY	H.H.S.
VILLEROY	4.4.18		Reorganisation	H.H.S.
	5.4.18		Reorganisation. Baths.	H.H.S.
	6.4.18		Reorganisation. Baths. Daily Routine	H.H.S.
	7.4.18		Daily Routine	H.H.S.
	8.4.18		Daily Routine. 'D' Coy. disbanded and divided among 'A', 'B' and 'C' Coys. A composite Coy. from 66th Div. arrived and was taken on the strength of the battalion as 'D' Coy. Strength of new Coy. 10 officers, 183 O.R's.	H.H.S.
	9.4.18	2p.m.	The battalion proceeded by march route to GAMACHES area. Bn. HQ and 'C' Coy were billetted for the night at RIEUX, 'A' Coy. at INCHVILLE, 'B' Coy. at BAZINVILLE, and 'D' Coy. at MONCHAUX.	H.H.S.
	10.4.18	4a.m.	The battalion marched by Companies to GAMACHES for entrainment to	

D. D. & L., London, E.C.
(A8204) Wt W1771/M2031 750,000 5/17 Sch. 52 Forms/C2118/14

Army Form C. 2118.

WAR DIARY
or
~~INTELLIGENCE SUMMARY.~~
(Erase heading not required.)

Instructions regarding War Diaries and Intelligence Summaries are contained in F. S. Regs., Part II. and the Staff Manual respectively. Title pages will be prepared in manuscript.

Place	Date	Hour	Summary of Events and Information	Remarks and references to Appendices
Ref. sheet FRANCE 36A	10.4.18.		CALONNE. First train with HQ, 'C' Coy and 'D' Coy left at 10 a.m. Second train with A Coy. and B. Coy. left at 1 p.m. First train arrived at CALONNE 12 midnight. The battalion was placed at the disposal of the 51st Division	H.H.S
	11.4.18	2.30 a.m.	'C' and 'D' Companies moved off to LE CORNET MALO by order of the 51st Division. Bn. HQ remained in CALONNE.	
		4.30 a.m.	Second train arrived at CALONNE. 'A' and 'B' Coys. occupied tents in the village.	
		5.0 a.m.	'C' and 'D' Coys. arrived at LE CORNET MALO. Both companies were placed at the disposal of G.O.C. 153 Bde. Immediately on arrival by order of 153 Bde. the whole of 'D' Coy's. guns were pushed up to a line East of PACAUT Q.23.d. central to Q.12.b. central to assist in stopping an enemy attack which was then in progress. 8 guns of 'C' Coy. took up a line running along road from PACAUT to Q.30.a. ~~[illegible]~~. 1 officer was sent to 153 Bde. HQ as Liaison Officer. These guns were in position at 6.45 a.m. 'D' Coy took over two of 'C' Coy's guns.	
		8.50 a.m.	1 officer and 4 guns of 'C' Coy. were sent to report to Bde. Major 153 Bde at PACAUT. These guns were immediately put into position on a line running from Q.17.d.4.3. to Q.17.b.51. A further two guns of 'C' Coy were	
		12.30 p.m.	Sent up to strengthen line East of LESTREM were in position at 12.30 p.m.	
		11.15 a.m.	'B' Coy. under orders of G.O.C. 152 Bde. moved off to take up positions in	

D. D. & L., London, E.C. (A8004) Wt W1771/M2031 750,000 5/17 Sch. 52 Forms/C2118/14

Army Form C. 2118.

WAR DIARY
or
~~INTELLIGENCE SUMMARY~~.
(Erase heading not required.)

Instructions regarding War Diaries and Intelligence Summaries are contained in F. S. Regs., Part II. and the Staff Manual respectively. Title pages will be prepared in manuscript.

Place	Date	Hour	Summary of Events and Information	Remarks and references to Appendices
	11.4.18	(Cont.)	Support to the main line in and about the Northern half of PACAUT WOOD. Three sections were used for this operation; one was held in reserve near Coy HQ, which was at Q.26.b.6.0. The move was	
Ref. Sheet FRANCE 36A 1/40,000		4.0 p.m.	completed at 4.0 p.m.	
			404 Field Coy. R.E. assisted 'B' Coy. as infantry.	
			Of 'A' Coy, two sections remained at CALONNE, and two Sections were sent into action on the left front under orders of 153 Bde. The	
		5.15 p.m.	move was complete at 5.15 p.m.	
		10 a.m.	Bn. HQ and Transport moved to Farm on the road, 1 Km. west of ROBECQ	
		6.30 p.m.	Transport moved a short distance West of the canal towards BUSNES.	
			At the end of the day the situation was as follows:	
			The line ran Q5 central, Q17 central, Q23 central, Q.29.d.9.2., Q.36.b.8.9. R.31.a.4.0., X.2. central.	
			'A' Coy. had 8 guns in the line with 153 Bde. 8 guns in reserve.	
			'B' Coy. " {12 guns " " " 152 Bde. {4 guns " reserve " "	
			'C' Coy " 12 guns in the line " 153 Bde.	Casualty 1 O.R. K.in A. J.H.S.
			'D' Coy. " {13 guns in the line " " " {5 " " reserve " " "	

D. D. & L., London, E.C.
(A8204) Wt W1771/M2031 750,000 5/17 Sch. 52 Forms/C2118/14

Instructions regarding War Diaries and Intelligence Summaries are contained in F. S. Regs., Part II. and the Staff Manual respectively. Title pages will be prepared in manuscript.

WAR DIARY
or
INTELLIGENCE SUMMARY.
(Erase heading not required.)

Army Form C. 2118.

Place	Date	Hour	Summary of Events and Information	Remarks and references to Appendices
1st. FRANCE 36 A 1/40000	12.4.8.	5.a.m.	The enemy attacked on the Divnl. Front. Parties of Germans had worked well inside our lines in the darkness. Their officers fired Very Lights on horseback. Bde. HQ came under rifle fire before daylight. Of 'A' Coy 2 guns with their teams were captured or destroyed by the enemy. The left front line section suffered this loss, and one gun which was moved by it's gun team commander was lost sight of. The remaining gun which lacked a tripod was therefore withdrawn. The other front line section, which was supplied with new guns which worked badly, was relieved by one of the reserve sections. The latter came into action in Q.9.a. after waiting till all infantry had passed it retired by sub-sections to Q.8.c. where it took up positions in co-operation with infantry, till recalled at 10.45 a.m. by Lt. HIGGINBOTTOM	
		10.a.m.	Lt. Higginbottom, who was in charge of the reserve half of 'A' Coy. was joined by 3 guns of 'C' Coy and 4 of 'D' Coy. which had all fired off all their ammunition and had returned for a further supply. On the return of the abovementioned reserve section, finding that the retirement of the	
		12.30.p.m.	infantry had left him in front of the front line, he succeeded in withdrawing all his personnel and limbers to the comparative safety of St VENANT. He then placed himself and his guns at the disposal of the G.O.C. 153 Inf. Bde., who held all 15 guns in reserve. Of 'B' Coy. HQ and the reserve section withdrew to P.36.a., when the infantry had all gone past. The reserve section took up position here. 7 guns had got away after the infantry left and were in position on both sides of the canal further East. The reserve section was shortly strengthened by 1 gun of 'A' Coy. and 2 guns of 'D' Coy, which	

D. D & L., London, E.C.
(A8604) Wt W1771/M2031 750,000 5/17 Sch. 52 Forms/C2118/14

Instructions regarding War Diaries and Intelligence Summaries are contained in F. S. Regs., Part II. and the Staff Manual respectively. Title pages will be prepared in manuscript.

WAR DIARY

or

~~INTELLIGENCE SUMMARY.~~

(Erase heading not required.)

Army Form C. 2118.

Place	Date	Hour	Summary of Events and Information	Remarks and references to Appendices
Ref. FRANCE 36 A 1/40000	12.4.18	(Contd.)	protected the infantry retirement from Q.31.a. One gun under 2/Lt ROWLAND also found it's way back, and joined the seven with 2/Lt. BARTHELEMY. A further two guns having lost their officer, and fired all their ammunition reached the Transport Lines.	
			All 'C' Coy's. guns retired by stages, swinging South West,	
		12 pm	and finally establishing themselves along the Southern bank of the canal between HINGES and ROBECQ, except the 3 guns of the left section, which have been mentioned above as having reported to Lt. HIGGINBOTTOM without ammunition. One gun was blown up with it's Limber, and one reached L'ECLEME. The latter was sent back to the Transport Lines in reserve.	
			Owing to casualties among the officers, 'D' Coy. became even more scattered than the others. Four guns were captured or destroyed in the first rush. Four missed their direction altogether, and were sent down by another Division to the Corps reinforcement Camp. Four reported to Lt. HIGGINBOTTOM without ammunition. One was picked up by 2/Lt Corrall, 'C' Coy., and kept in action by him. The five reserve guns were formed into a composite Coy. under Capt. GILBERT, comdg. D Coy., together with Lt. HENDERSON'S 4 guns, and 1 gun of 'C' Coy., sent up from the transport.	
		12.30 pm.	This composite Coy. was formed at 12.30 p.m. and was disposed according to orders brought by a 3rd Bn. M.G.C. Coy. Comdr. from his	

D. D. & L., London, E.C.
(A8004) Wt W1771/M2031 750,000 5/17 Sch. 52 Forms/C2118/14

Army Form C. 2118.

Instructions regarding War Diaries and Intelligence Summaries are contained in F. S. Regs., Part II. and the Staff Manual respectively. Title pages will be prepared in manuscript.

WAR DIARY
or
~~INTELLIGENCE SUMMARY.~~

(Erase heading not required.)

Place	Date	Hour	Summary of Events and Information	Remarks and references to Appendices
Ref. FRANCE 36A 1/40000	12.4.18.	(Contd)	G.O.C. Brigade. In accordance with these orders the guns were distributed in and about P.36.a. for the defence of the bridge head.	
			In the afternoon Lieut. Mowatt, 2nd i/c of 'A' Coy., found Lt. HIGGINBOTTOM at HOLLANDERIE [P.20.c.] with 11 guns of 'A' Coy., 3 guns of 'C' Coy, & 4 guns of 'D' Coy. He went and found Capt. Rothwell + Lt. Evans, O.C. 'C' Coy. at the bridge in P.36.a., whither they had arrived after fighting their way back each with 1 reserve gun of 'D' Coy. These two guns were included in the 5 guns of 'D' Coy. in Capt. GILBERT'S Composite Coy. When Capt. Rothwell learned this information, He went & took over the 18 guns from Lt. HIGGINBOTTOM.	
		6p.m.	At night 'C' Coy. and Capt. Rothwell's Composite Coy. were ordered to withdraw their guns and concentrate at P.22.c.6.3.; where they were to join ~~Col.~~ FLEMING'S FORCE, and come under the orders of Col. Fleming who commanded it. The Force was organised for the defence of a line from P.36.a.4.8 to P.17.d.4.9. and was under orders of 5th Div:	
			At this time the Bn. had 43 guns organised for action: Two composite Coys. of 18 guns and 10 guns respectively, eight guns of 'B' Coy., and 7 guns of 'C' Coy. including the one gun of 'D' Coy., picked up by 2/Lt. Corrall.	H.H.J.
			Casualties Lieut. C.V. BOOTH, W. in A. O.R. 15 W. in A " 14 Missing	
	13.4.18.		Lieut. Evans, O.C. 'C' Coy., having no one who knew where 'C' Coy's guns were, set out to find them himself on the night of the 12th/13th. This he was unable to do, owing to the extreme darkness. He was therefore unable to take his guns to Fleming's Force. Not having found them at 2.30.a.m. 13th	

D. D & L., London, E.C. (A8304) Wt W1771/M2031 750,000 5/17 Sch. 52 Forms/C2118/14

Army Form C. 2118.

Instructions regarding War Diaries and Intelligence Summaries are contained in F. S. Regs., Part II. and the Staff Manual respectively. Title pages will be prepared in manuscript.

WAR DIARY
or
~~INTELLIGENCE SUMMARY.~~

(Erase heading not required.)

Place	Date	Hour	Summary of Events and Information	Remarks and references to Appendices
Ref. FRANCE 36A 1/40000	13.4.18	9.15am	he informed the C.O. of the Bn. and decided to wait till daylight. At 9.a.m. orders were received to withdraw all guns to HAM EN ARTOIS. During the afternoon all guns except the eighteen under Capt. ROTHWELL were withdrawn to Transport LINES near HAM EN ARTOIS. During the night of 12th/13th 10 of Capt. ROTHWELLS guns were pushed up into the line, and eight held in reserve.	H.H.S.
HAM EN ARTOIS	14.4.18		Guns out of line – Reorganisation etc. Casualties O.Rs 1 K.in A, 3 W.in A, 6 Missing Guns in line – Dispositions unchanged.	H.H.S.
"	15.4.18.		Guns out of line – Organisation of Gun Kit etc. Guns in line – Relieved by 51st Bn. M.G. Corps – Relief Complete 1.0 p.m.	H.H.S.
"	16.4.18.		The battalion was placed under orders of 61st Div.	H.H.S.
"	17.4.18.		Composite Coy. formed of 'C' Coy. 8 guns and 'D' Coy. 8 guns with Lt Evans in command and Lt. Keenan, 2 i/c D.Coy, as second i/c, took over 10 gun positions from 8th Cav. M.G Squadron on a line roughly co-incident with the St VENANT – ROBECQ Road. Two guns were held in reserve at Coy. HQ [The Lock P.4.b] and four at the Transport Lines [HARTE VENTE]	H.H.S.

Army Form C. 2118.

WAR DIARY
or
~~INTELLIGENCE SUMMARY.~~
(Erase heading not required.)

Instructions regarding War Diaries and Intelligence Summaries are contained in F. S. Regs., Part II. and the Staff Manual respectively. Title pages will be prepared in manuscript.

Place	Date	Hour	Summary of Events and Information	Remarks and references to Appendices
Ref. FRANCE 36A 1/40000 HAMENARTOIS	18.4.18 19.4.18 20.4.18		Composite Coy. in the line. Remainder - Daily Routine. Casualties O.R's. 2 W. in A.	H. H. S.
	21.4.18		'B' Coy. with 14 guns and 2 guns of 'D' Coy. relieved the Composite Coy. in the line	H. H. S.
	22.4.18 23.4.18 24.4.18		'B' Coy. in Line. Remainder Daily Routine. Casualty O.R. 1 W. in A. (gassed) " O.R. 1 " " " O.R. 6 " "	H. H. S.
	25.4.18		'A' Coy. relieved 'B' Coy. with 12 guns; 10 in the line, 2 in Reserve. Relief complete 9.20 p.m.	H. H. S.
	26.4.18		'D' Coy relieved 12 guns of 51st Bn. M. G. Corps with 12 guns. Two res. guns of 'A' Coy. withdrawn	H. H. S.
	27.4.18 28.4.18 29.4.18		Daily Routine Casualty - 1. O.R. Wounded in Action	H. H. S. H. H. S. H. H. S.
	30.4.18		'C' Coy. relieved 'D' Coy. in the line with 12 guns. Relief Complete 7.0 p.m.	H. H. S.

[signature]
Lt. Col.
Comdg. 39th Bn.
M. G. Corps.
1.5.18.

D. D. & L., London, E.C.
(A7001) Wt. W1771/M2031 750,000 5/17 Sch. 52 Forms/C2118/14

39th Divisional Troops

39th BATTALION

MACHINE GUN CORPS

M A Y 1 9 1 8

Vol 3

CONFIDENTIAL

WAR DIARY
of
39th Bn. Machine Gun Corps
from May 1st to May 31st, 1918

Volume III

Instructions regarding War Diaries and Intelligence Summaries are contained in F. S. Regs., Part II. and the Staff Manual respectively. Title pages will be prepared in manuscript.

WAR DIARY
or
~~INTELLIGENCE SUMMARY~~.
(Erase heading not required.)

Army Form C. 2118.

Place	Date	Hour	Summary of Events and Information	Remarks and references to Appendices
Ref. Map FRANCE 36A 1/40000	May 1st		'A' Coy. had ten guns, 'C' Coy. 12 guns in the LES AMUSOIRES—HAVERSKERQUE LINE from J 35.c. to P.36.a. Remainder at HAM EN ARTOIS – Daily Routine – Gun work and Physical Drill etc.	H.H.S.
HAM EN ARTOIS	May 2nd		'B' Coy. relieved 'A' Coy. with 10 guns. Relief Complete 8.10 p.m. Daily Routine. Reinforcements: 44 O.R.	H.H.S.
	May 3rd, May 4th, May 5th		Daily Routine.	H.H.S. H.H.S. H.H.S.
	May 6th	9.55a.m.	Casualty: 1 O.R. wounded. 'D' Coy moved off to be attached to 5th Divn. for digging emplacements in the MORBECQ Line from J.34.a. to J.3.d. Composite Coy. 4 guns each of A, B, & C Coys under Capt. MOWAT relieved the 12 guns of 'C' Coy in the line. Reinforcements: Lieut. W. STOTT. M.C., " E. BOOTH, T/2/Lt. G.R. JAMSON, T/2/Lt. E. CLAYTON, " A. MALKIN, " W.G. GUTHRIE	H.H.S.
	May 7th		Daily Routine. Training of att'd Infantry transferred Infantry from P.20.d to P.28 d.	H.H.S.
	May 8th		'C' Coy. was allotted positions on the AIRE CANAL SWITCH LINE to be occupied on receipt of order 'MAN BATTLE STATIONS'.	H.H.S.
	May 9th		Training as under May 7th. 'A' Coy. relieved 'B' Coy in the line with 10 guns. 12 midnight 2 guns at P.18.c. 00.75 transferred from command of O.C. Composite Coy. to command of O.C. 'A' Coy. Relief Complete 7.55 p.m. Casualty: 1 O.R. wounded.	H.H.S.
	May 10th		Guns in line – Trench Routine	H.H.S.
	May 11th		Training as under May 7th — Casualty: 1 O.R. wounded — Reinforcement a/Maj. A.N. RICHARDSON	H.H.S.
	May 12th		Guns out of line – Daily Routine. 'B' Coy. took over the task of 'C' Coy.	H.H.S.

D. D. & L., London, E.C. (A8204) Wt W1771/M2031 750,000 5/17 Sch. 52 Forms/C2118/14

Army Form C. 2118.

WAR DIARY
or
~~INTELLIGENCE~~ SUMMARY.
(Erase heading not required.)

Instructions regarding War Diaries and Intelligence Summaries are contained in F. S. Regs., Part II. and the Staff Manual respectively. Title pages will be prepared in manuscript.

Place	Date	Hour	Summary of Events and Information	Remarks and references to Appendices
Ref. map FRANCE 36A 1/40000 HAM EN ARTOIS	May 13th		'C' Coy. with 12 guns relieved the Composite Coy. and 2 guns of 'A' Coy. Relief Complete 7 p.m. The Composite Company on reaching Bn. HQ. was dissolved. At 12 midnight the 2 guns at P.18.a.00.75. were transferred from command of O.C. 'A' Coy. to command of O.C. 'C' Coy.	
			Training as under May 7th.	H.H.S.
	May 14th		Daily Routine. Training as under May 7th.	H.H.S.
	May 15th		A Composite Coy. under Capt. R. W. FYFFE was formed with one section each of 'A' 'B' + 'C' Coys., and one section ~~[illegible]~~ composed of 2 guns of 'A' Coy. + 2 guns of school of instruction for attached men. It took over the task of 'D' Coy. at 12 noon. Reinforcements: 2. O.R.	H.H.S.
	May 16th		'B' Coy (10 guns) relieved the 10 guns of 'A' Coy. in the line. Relief complete. Training, Routine + School of instruction.	H.H.S.
	May 17th May 18th		Training and Routine.	H.H.S. H.H.S.
	May 19th		'A' Coy. took over the task of the Composite Coy. at 12 noon. Reinforcements { T/Lt. S.G.F. DOLLEY, Lt. E. DANE, Lt. G.W. GOODMAN + 1. O.R.	H.H.S.
	May 20th		Composite Coy. (12 guns) took over the line from 'C' Coy (12 guns) Relief Complete 7.10 p.m.	
			Battalion allotted to First Army as Army Machine Gun Battalion	H.H.S.
	May 21st		The 22 guns in the line were relieved by 16 guns of the 61st Bn. M.G.C. All companies, including 'D' Coy. concentrated at HAM EN ARTOIS. The Composite Coy. was automatically disbanded on relief.	
	May 22nd		The battalion moved into Army Reserve at ROMBLY. HQ N.21.d.85.60. move complete at 11.30. a.m.	H.H.S.

D. D. & L., London, E.C.
(A5001) Wt. W1 71/M2031 750,000 5/17 Sch. 52 Forms/C2.118/14

Army Form C. 2118.

Instructions regarding War Diaries and Intelligence Summaries are contained in F. S. Regs., Par. II, and the Staff Manual respectively. Title pages will be prepared in manuscript.

WAR DIARY
or
~~INTELLIGENCE~~ ~~SUMMARY~~.
(Erase heading not required.)

Place	Date	Hour	Summary of Events and Information	Remarks and references to Appendices
Ref. map FRANCE 36 A 1/40000 ROMBLY	May 23rd		Reorganisation of Gun Kit etc. Reinforcements 36 O.R.	H.H.S.
	May 24th			
	May 25th		Reinforcements 20 O.R.	H.H.S.
	May 26th			
	May 27th		Training. N.C.O's Course: M.G. Course including miniature Range:	
	May 28th		Rangetakers' + Scouts' Course. Reinforcement 1 O.R. (May 27th)	H.H.S.
	May 29th			
	May 30th			
	May 31st		Reinforcements Capt. H.K. BOYLE T/Lt. E.J. HODGSON T/Lt. G.N. BLAIR	H.H.S.
			[signature] Lieut. Col. Commanding 39th Battalion Machine Gun Corps.	
			31.5.18.	

A6945 Wt. W11422/M1160 350,000 12/16 D. D. & L. Forms/C./2118/14.

4

CONFIDENTIAL.

WAR DIARY

of

39th BATTALION MACHINE GUN CORPS.

JUNE 1st 1918 to JUNE 30th 1918

VOLUME IV.

Instructions regarding War Diaries and Intelligence Summaries are contained in F. S. Regs., Part II. and the Staff Manual respectively. Title pages will be prepared in manuscript.

WAR DIARY
or
~~INTELLIGENCE SUMMARY.~~
(Erase heading not required.)

39TH BATTALION, MACHINE GUN CORPS.
No. 39/MG/W/111
Date 3/7/18

Army Form C. 2118.

Place	Date	Hour	Summary of Events and Information	Remarks and references to Appendices
Ref. Sheet FRANCE 36 A 1/40000	1.6.18.		Reconnoitring 1st Army and XIth and XIIIth Corps lines by motor 'bus May 23rd to June 3rd.	
	2.6.18		Training. N.C.O's., M.G., and Rangetakers	
ROMBLY	3.6.18	–	Reconnaisance of 1st Army and XI and XIII Corps lines completed.	RHL
		2.30pm	Inspection by C.O. of each coy. in drill order. Training. N.C.O^s. M.G. and rangetakers	
	4.6.18	3 pm	Inspection by Major Richardson (second in command) of gun equipment of "A" and "C" Coys. Training – N.C.O^s, M.G., ~~and~~ Rangetakers, and Scouts.	RHL
	5.6.18	3pm	Inspection of "B" and "D" Coys. gun equipment. Training – N.C.O^s. M.G. Rangetakers + Scouts	RHL
	6.6.18		Training as on June 5.	RHL
	7.6.18		Training as on June 5. Reinforcements arrived – 9 O.R.	RHL
	8.6.18	9 am	Reconnaisance of G.H.Q. Line by motor-bus commenced. Training as on June 5	RHL
	9.6.18		Nil	RHL
	10.6.18	9.0am	Reconnaisance and Training as on June 8.	RHL
	11.6.18	9.0am	Reconnaisance and Training as on June 8	RHL
	12.6.18	11.30am	Exhibition of M.G. work photographed by the official photographer. Photographs were taken of (1) A.A. firing (4) Section's Gun Kit laid out for inspection (2) Emplacement up a tree (5) M.G. nest – study in concealment (7) Galloping into action on limbers (3) Transport lines (6) Range work in gas masks Reinforcements – 20 O.R.	RHL
	13.6.18	11.30am	G.O.C. 1st Army inspected the battalion in full marching order. The battalion was drawn up in line, gave the general salute, was inspected and then marched past. The camp was inspected afterwards. The G.O.C. expressed himself extraordinarily pleased with all he had seen.	RHL

D. D. & L., London, E.C.
(A10266) Wt W5300/P713 750,000 2/18 Sch. 52 Forms/C2118/16

Army Form C. 2118.

WAR DIARY
or
INTELLIGENCE SUMMARY.
(Erase heading not required.)

Instructions regarding War Diaries and Intelligence Summaries are contained in F. S. Regs., Part II. and the Staff Manual respectively. Title pages will be prepared in manuscript.

Place	Date	Hour	Summary of Events and Information	Remarks and references to Appendices
Ref. Sheet FRANCE 36 A 1/40.000. ROMBLY	13·6·18	12 Noon	Two companies were ordered to be sent to come under the command of O.C. 5th Batt. M.G.C. The companies detailed were "B" and "C" Major L.W. Evans M.C. being in charge. He was ordered to ~~more~~ [more] with his command to 5th Battn. M.G.C. H.Q. (I 20 c 7.2) on 14·6·18.	R.H.L.
	14·6·18	9.0am	Training and Reconnaisance for "A" and "D" companies, as on June 8. Reinforcements arrived 2/Lieut W.B. Pickles 2/Lieut E.R. Pike and 1 O.R.	R.H.L.
		1 pm	Major L.W. Evans M.C. started from camp with his command, and reached PECQUEUR at 4pm, where all were soon comfortably installed in billets.	
			It was found that "B" and "C" Coys were detailed to assist the 5th Battn. M.G.C. in local	
		5.30pm	operations by barrage fire. Accordingly at 5.30 pm Major Evans M.C. Capt. Boyle, Capt. Hooper, Lt. Henderson M.C. Lt Stunt, Lt Hall and Lt Hodgson set out to reconnoitre the line under the second-in-command of the 5th Battn, Major Kidd.	
			Four batteries were to be manned by us, forming the right group of the barrage. The battery positions were sited as follows:–	R.H.L.
			"D" Battery K 14 b 7,0 — 1 and 3 sections "C" Coy. under Lt Hall	
			"E" Battery K 14 b 50,65 — 2 and 4 sections "C" Coy. under Lt Stunt	
			"F" Battery K 9 c 9,8 — 1 and 2 Sections "B" Coy. under Lt Hodgson	
			"G" Battery K 9 a 70,65 — 3 and 4 Sections "B" Coy. under Lt Henderson M.C.	
	15·6·18	10.30am	A Cinematographer arrived from the war correspondents H.Q. to take films of M.G. work. The following pictures were taken: (1) An M.G. Section going into the trenches, using pack animals. (2) An M.G. position in a tree (3) The alarm is given, and the team rush to their places. (4) Mule wrestling. (5) Officers playing Quoit tennis. (6) M.G.s practising A.A. firing. (7) An M.G. section returning to camp after a tour of duty in the line	R.H.L.

D. D. & L., London, E.C.
(A10266) Wt W5300/P713 750,000 2/18 Sch. 52 Forms/C2118/16

Army Form C. 2118.

Instructions regarding War Diaries and Intelligence Summaries are contained in F. S. Regs., Part II. and the Staff Manual respectively. Title pages will be prepared in manuscript.

WAR DIARY
or
~~INTELLIGENCE SUMMARY.~~

(Erase heading not required.)

Place	Date	Hour	Summary of Events and Information	Remarks and references to Appendices
Ref. Sheet FRANCE 36a 1/40,000. LA PECQUEUR I20 c	15.6.18	9.0am - noon	"B" and "C" Coys were employed overhauling guns and belts	
		8 pm.	Working parties from "B" and "C" proceeded by light railway from Hanston station I29 a 0.5 to K 13 b 5,8, and thence at dusk to battery positions, which were dug and camouflaged; 8 "T" bases were also put in by each coy. These parties returned at 4 am. 16.6.18.	P.H.L.
ROMBLY	16.6.18	10.30am	The cinematographer arrived, but the weather was unsuitable; further arrangements were made for 17.6.18.	P.H.L.
LA PECQUEUR		10.0am - noon.	"B" and "C" - practice in use of traversing and elevating dial; overhauling of belts. Fighting maps, group and battery charts prepared in accordance with O.O.8 of 5th Battn. M.G.C.	P.H.L.
		8 pm.	Parties proceeded by train to battery positions, which were completed; the remaining "T" bases were put in.	P.H.L.
ROMBLY	17.6.18	10.30AM.	Cinematographer arrived. Picture taken - (1) A rearguard action - 2 guns cover the retirement of the other two guns of their section. (2) An M.G. nest. (2 guns.) (3) An M.G. section galloping into action. (4) Four M.G.s knock down a sandbag wall 18 ins. thick. (5) M.G.s and infantry repel an attack. (6) Stripping a gun.	P.H.L.
LA PECQUEUR		9.30am - noon.	"B" and "C" Coys - Rehearsal of barrages	
ROMBLY.	18.6.18	9.0am.	Reconnaissance of G.H.Q. line continued.	
		9.0pm.	G.H.Q. Photographer arrived and took the follow[ing] eight photographs of M.G. work. (1) An M.G. subsection galloping into action (2) It pulls up (3) Taking ammunition to a position in a tree.	P.H.L.

D. D. & L., London, E.C.
(A10266) Wt W5300/P713 750,000 2/18 Sch. 52 Forms/C2118/16

Army Form C. 2118.

Instructions regarding War Diaries and Intelligence Summaries are contained in F. S. Regs., Part II. and the Staff Manual respectively. Title pages will be prepared in manuscript.

WAR DIARY
or
~~INTELLIGENCE SUMMARY.~~

(*Erase heading not required.*)

Place	Date	Hour	Summary of Events and Information	Remarks and references to Appendices
Ref Sheet FRANCE 36 A 1/40,000 ROMBLY.	18.6.18	9.0 pm	④ A team going into the line. ⑤ A subsection in action ⑥ A subsection climbing up a bank into action.	[initials]
18.6. LA PECQUEUR		8 pm	Working parties of "B" and "C" prepared for barrage. 24 belt-boxes per gun were carried up, and two dumps of 50,000 rounds SAA were formed. Water, and gas solution was brought up, and zero lines laid out.	[initials]
ROMBLY	19.6.18	9.0 am	Reconnaissance of G.H.Q. Line.	
LA PECQUEUR		10 pm	Operations were postponed indefinitely. All belt boxes were withdrawn from the position.	[initials]
ROMBLY	20.6.18	9.0 am	Reconnaissance as on June 19.	
		4.30 pm	"B" and "C" coys arrived from LA PECQUEUR	[initials]
	21.6.18	9.0 am	Reconnaissance as on June 20. Training - M.G., N.C.Os, Rangetakers and Scouts classes were recommenced.	[initials]
	22.6.18	9.0 am	Reconnaissance and training as on June 21.	[initials]
	23.6.18		Nothing to report. Reinforcements arrived - 1 o.r.	[initials]
	24.6.18	9.0 am	Reconnaissance and training as on June 21. Orders were received for two companies to be again attached to 5th Bn. M.G.C.	[initials]
	25.6.18	9.0 am	Reconnaissance and training as on June 24.	[initials]
LA PECQUEUR			"B" and "C" Coys, which had been detailed ~~to~~ in accordance with orders received on the 24th inst. moved off under command of Major L.W. Evans M.C. Proceeding by march route, these coys. arrived at H.Q. 5 Batt. M.G.C. at 11 am. and were allotted the same billets they had occupied 14 - 19th inst.	[initials]

D. D. & L., London, E.C.
(A10266) Wt W5300/P713 750,000 2/18 Sch. 52 Forms/C2118/16

Army Form C. 2118.

WAR DIARY
or
~~INTELLIGENCE SUMMARY.~~
(Erase heading not required.)

Instructions regarding War Diaries and Intelligence Summaries are contained in F. S. Regs., Part II. and the Staff Manual respectively. Title pages will be prepared in manuscript.

Place	Date	Hour	Summary of Events and Information	Remarks and references to Appendices
Ref. Sheet FRANCE 36 A 1/40,000.	25.6.18	2.30pm	The afternoon was spent preparing all gun kit for the line.	PhhL
LA PECQUEUR. ROMBLY	26.6.18	9.0am	Reconnaissance and training as on June 25. A considerable number of cases of influenza had occurred in the battalion. A barn was therefore set aside for the sick men; blankets were obtained for them and a special diet was prepared; the barn was also isolated.	PhhL
LA PECQUEUR		7pm	All gun kit, water and accessories were taken up to the battery positions by "B" and "C" Coys. Four batteries were being manned by these Coys; they were distributed as follows: "D" Battery K 14 b 7.0 — 1 and 3 sections "C" Coy. under Lt Hall. "E" Battery K 14 b 50,65. — 2 and 4 sections "C" Coy. under Lt Stint and Lt Dane "F" Battery K 9 c 9,8. — 1 and 2 sections "B" Coy. under Lt Hodgson and Lt Bartelemy. G Battery K 9 a 70.65. — 3 and 4 sections "B" Coy. under Lt Henderson M.C and 2/Lt Guthrie. All preparations for barrage were completed and all zero posts laid out. 1 N.C.O and two men, together with the officers mentioned above with the exception of Lt Hodgson and Lt Henderson M.C. remained at the positions	PhhL

D. D. & L., London, E.C.
(A10266) Wt W5300/P713 750,000 2/18 Sch. 52 Forms/C2118/16

Army Form C. 2118.

Instructions regarding War Diaries and Intelligence Summaries are contained in F. S. Regs., Part II. and the Staff Manual respectively. Title pages will be prepared in manuscript.

WAR DIARY
or
~~INTELLIGENCE SUMMARY.~~

(Erase heading not required.)

Place	Date	Hour	Summary of Events and Information	Remarks and references to Appendices
Ref. Sheet FRANCE 36 A 1/40,000. ROMBLY LA PECQUEUR.	27.6.18	9.0am.	Reconnaisance as on June 25.	
		7pm.	The remainder of personnel in "B" and "C" Coys marched up and manned the battery positions. By 10.30 pm all guns were laid on their first target of the barrage. All batteries were connected up by phone to Group H.Q from which a line ran on 13th Bde. H.Q. Group H.Q. was at K 14 b 65,95. These batteries thus found themselves in position ready to cover the advance of the 13th Inf. Bde, whose objective was a line running from K 15 a 55,88 – K16 c 39,95, – K10 d 4.0 – K 10 d 80,45 – road junction K 11 b 5,8. A creeping barrage was to be put down during the attack, and a protective barrage applied to cover part of the consolidation. Afterwards the guns were to be laid on S.O.S. lines. The Zero hour was notified to be 6.0 am.	RHL
	28.6.18	6AM.	Zero – the artillery opened out, – at zero +1 the batteries opened fire and proceeded according to the pre-arranged programme. The attack went forward without a hitch and all objectives were gained well within scheduled time. At 7.41 the guns ceased fire and laid on S.O.S. lines. Retaliation had been very slight, but the batteries had been unlucky and had lost Lt H.H Henderson M.C. wounded, 4 O.R.s ~~wounded~~ killed and 10 R. wounded. The command of "G" Battery therefore devolved on Lt Bartelemy.	RHL

D. D. & L., London, E.C.
(A10266) Wt W5300/P713 750,000 2/18 Sch. 52 Forms/C2118/16

Instructions regarding War Diaries and Intelligence Summaries are contained in F. S. Regs., Part II. and the Staff Manual respectively. Title pages will be prepared in manuscript.

WAR DIARY
or
~~INTELLIGENCE SUMMARY.~~
(Erase heading not required.)

Army Form C. 2118.

Place	Date	Hour	Summary of Events and Information	Remarks and references to Appendices
Ref Sheet FRANCE 36A 1/40,000. K9, 14	28.6.18	4.30pm	Situation quietened down until the afternoon, when some desultory shelling took place, which increased very much on the left until the S.O.S. was put up at 4.38 pm. The guns immediately opened out, but ceased fire again at 4.55 pm, as the counter attack had been very weak and had failed utterly. S.O.S calls were answered at 10.30 pm and 10.50 pm, but no infantry action developed.	Ph.h.h.
ROMBLY		~~9 am~~	Nothing to report.	Ph.h.h.
K9. 14	29.6.18	MIDNIGHT	Gas shells were freely used and S.B.R.s were worn until 3.30 am. 3 O.R.s were sent down gassed.	
		8.45am	Enemy artillery became very active, but no infantry action developed. Our artillery replied and a duel was kept up till noon.	Ph.h.h.
ROMBLY			Nothing to report.	Ph.h.h.
K9, 14	30.6.18	3.30am	S.O.S. call was answered, but no infantry action followed.	
		10 pm	Withdrawal was commenced – 16 belt boxes per gun were sent away, and positions were cleared up.	Ph.h.h.
ROMBLY	3		Nothing to report 13 O.R.s – reinforcements – arrived.	Ph.h.h.

A. Richardson
Major
Commdg 39 Batt. M.G.C.

D. D. & L., London, E.C.
(A10265) Wt W5300/P713 750,000 2/16 Sch. 52 Forms/C2118/16

CONFIDENTIAL.

WAR DIARY

- OF -

39th (ARMY) MACHINE GUN BATTALION.

FROM 1st JULY 1918 TO 31st JULY 1918.

VOLUME V.

oOo

Instructions regarding War Diaries and Intelligence Summaries are contained in F. S. Regs., Part II. and the Staff Manual respectively. Title pages will be prepared in manuscript.

WAR DIARY
or
~~INTELLIGENCE~~ SUMMARY.
(Erase heading not required.)

39TH BATTALION, MACHINE GUN CORPS.
No. ....
Date ....

Army Form C. 2118.

Place	Date	Hour	Summary of Events and Information	Remarks and references to Appendices
Ref Sheet FRANCE 36 A 1/40.000				
ROMBLY	1.7.18	9.0am	M.G. Training. Reinforcements arrived - 134 O.R.	RDhL
K 9. 14		10.30pm	"B" and "C" Coys commenced withdrawal from battery positions: the transport arrived at 11pm and all gun kit was loaded on to it. At 11.30 pm "C" left on light railway train for PECQUEOR, followed at midnight by "B" Coy	RDhL
ROMBLY	2.7.18	9.0am	M.G. Training. Reinforcements arrived - 9 O.R.	RDhL
LA PECQUEOR		2.30am	"B" and "C" Coys left by march route for ROMBLY, arriving at 4.30 pm.	RDhL
ROMBLY	3.7.18	9.0am	M.G. Training.	RDhL
	4.7.18	9.0am	Reconnaisance of G.H.Q. line continued by "B" & "C" Coys. Training in M.G. Schools of instruction commenced - (1) scouts (2) Rangefinders.	RDhL
	5.7.18	9.0am	Reconnaisance and Training as on 4th inst.	RDhL
	6.7.18	9.0am	Reconnaisance and Training as on 4th inst. An additional school of instruction was opened - a drill course for N.C.Os	RDhL
	7.7.18	-	Nothing to Report	RDhL
	8.7.18	9.0am	Reconnaisance and Training as on 6th inst. The front of the XIII Corps was extended south so as to include BETHUNE.	RDhL
	9.7.18	9.0am	Reconnaisance and Training as on 6th inst. Reinforcements arrived - 4 O.R.	RDhL

D. D. & L., London, E.C.
(A10266) Wt W5300/P713 750,000 2/18 Sch. 52 Forms/C2118/16

Army Form C. 2118.

Instructions regarding War Diaries and Intelligence Summaries are contained in F. S. Regs., Part II. and the Staff Manual respectively. Title pages will be prepared in manuscript.

WAR DIARY

or

~~INTELLIGENCE~~ SUMMARY.

(*Erase heading not required.*)

Place	Date	Hour	Summary of Events and Information	Remarks and references to Appendices
Ref. Sheet FRANCE 36A 1/40,000 ROMBLY	10·7·18	9·0am	Reconnaissance of the part of line taken over by XIII Corps (see diary for 8th inst.)	RWhL
			Training – N.C.O's M.G. rangetakers and Scouts.	
	11·7·18	9·0am	Reconnaissance as on 10th inst. Scouts school disbanded.	RWhL
			Training – N.C.O's M.G. and rangetakers.	RWhL
	12·7·18	9·0am	Reconnaissance and Training as on 11th inst.	RWhL
	13·7·18	9·0am	Reconnaissance and Training as on 11th inst.	RWhL
	14·7·18	9·0am	Reconnaissance and Training as on 11th inst.	RWhL
	15·7·18	9·0am	Reconnaissance and Training as on 11th inst.	RWhL
	16·7·18	9·0am	Reconnaissance and Training as on 11th inst.	RWhL
			Reinforcements arrived – 2 O.R.	RWhL
	17·7·18	9·0am	Reconnaissance and Training as on 11th inst.	RWhL
	18·7·18	9·0am	Reconnaissance and Training as on 11th inst.	RWhL
			Reinforcements arrived – 1 O.R.	RWhL
	19·7·18	9·0am	Reconnaissance and Training as on 11th inst.	RWhL
			Reinforcements arrived – 10 O.R.	RWhL
	20·7·18	9·0am	Reconnaissance as on 11th inst. N.C.O's school disbanded.	RWhL
			Training M.G. and rangetakers.	RWhL
	21·7·18	–	Nothing to report.	RWhL
	22·7·18	9·0am	Reconnaissance and Training as on 20th inst.	RWhL
	23·7·18	9·0am	Reconnaissance and Training as on 20th inst.	RWhL

D. D. & L., London, E.C.
(A10266) Wt W5300/P713 750,000 2/18 Sch. 52 Forms/C2118/16

Army Form C. 2118.

Instructions regarding War Diaries and Intelligence Summaries are contained in F. S. Regs., Part II. and the Staff Manual respectively. Title pages will be prepared in manuscript.

WAR DIARY
or
INTELLIGENCE SUMMARY.
(Erase heading not required.)

Place	Date	Hour	Summary of Events and Information	Remarks and references to Appendices
Ref. FRANCE SHEET 36A 1/40,000 ROMBLY	24.7.18	9.0am	Reconnaisance of Corps and Army Lines on Vth army front. Training M.G. and Rangetakers. Reinforcements arrived - 2 O.R.	[initials]
	25.7.18	9.0am	Reconnaisance as on 24th. Rangetaker school disbanded. Training M.G.	[initials]
	26.7.18	9.0am	Reconnaisance and Training as on 25th.	
H 7 c . d.	27.7.18	9.0am	Corps Horse Show took place. The battalion secured three 2nd places and one 3rd. Event 17 - Machine Gun Limbered Wagon - 2nd Event 19 - G.S. Wagon and Pair of Horses - 2nd Event 20. - Best H.D. horse - stripped - 2nd Event 14 - Battalion Transport - 3rd	[initials]
	28.7.18	9.0am	Reconnaisance of all rear lines of defence on Army front completed. Training as on 25th. Reinforcements arrived - 5 O.R.	[initials]
	29.7.18	9.0am	Training as on 25th - 1 officer arrived to act as Coy. Transport Officer on probation (2Lt. J. NEWELL)	[initials]
	30.7.18	9.0am	Training as on 25th.	[initials]
	31.7.18	9.0am	Battalion Scheme of intensive training commenced.	[initials]

A Fleetwood Wilson
Lt. Col.
Commdg. 39th (Army) Machine Gun Battalion.

D. D. & L., London, E.C.
(A10266) Wt W5300/P713 750,000 2/18 Sch. 52 Forms/C2118/16

9

Army Form C. 2118.

Instructions regarding War Diaries and Intelligence Summaries are contained in F. S. Regs., Part II. and the Staff Manual respectively. Title pages will be prepared in manuscript.

WAR DIARY
or
~~INTELLIGENCE SUMMARY.~~
(Erase heading not required.)

39 Bn M G Corps

Vol 6

Place	Date	Hour	Summary of Events and Information	Remarks and references to Appendices
Ref FRANCE Sheet 36A 1/40,000 ROMBLY	1.8.18	8.30am	Training according to Battalion Scheme of Intensive Training.	
	2.8.18	8.30am	Training as on 1st inst.	
	3.8.18	8.30am	Training as on 1st inst.	
	4.8.18	–	Nothing to report.	
	5.8.18	8.30am	Training as on 1st inst. Reinforcements arrived – 2/Lt Bell on probation as company transport officer.	
	6.8.18	11.30am	Two companies were placed under the orders of XI Corps – later in the day this order was changed to read the entire battalion.	
		11.30pm	Orders were issued by XI Corps that the battalion was attached to 61st Division to assist in the operation designated "PARTRIDGE" – the object of which was to capture the enemy's front line on the whole of the Corps front. 2 M.G. barrage maps were to be constructed and steps ~~were~~ taken to prepare the battalion to move on 24 hours notice.	
	7.8.18	9.0am	Preparations for "PARTRIDGE" were made.	
	8.8.18	2.40pm	All orders concerning PARTRIDGE were cancelled. Reinforcements arrived – 1 OR.	
	9.8.18	8.30am	Battalion Scheme of Intensive Training resumed.	
	10.8.18	8.30am	Training as on 9th inst.	
	11.8.18	–	Nothing to report.	

D. D. & L., London, E.C.
(A10266) Wt W5300/P713 750,000 2/18 Sch. 52 Forms/C2118/16

Army Form C. 2118.

Instructions regarding War Diaries and Intelligence Summaries are contained in F. S. Regs., Part II. and the Staff Manual respectively. Title pages will be prepared in manuscript.

WAR DIARY
~~or~~
INTELLIGENCE ~~SUMMARY~~.

(*Erase heading not required.*)

Place	Date	Hour	Summary of Events and Information	Remarks and references to Appendices
Ref. SHEET FRANCE 36A 1/40,000 ROMBLY	12.8.18	8.30am	Battalion Scheme of Intensive Training resumed.	PBLeh
	13.8.18	8.30am	Training as on 12th inst.	PBLeh
	14.8.18	8.30am	Training programme postponed. Preparation for inspection by G.O.C. V Army.	PBLeh
	15.8.18	11am	Battalion inspected by G.O.C. V Army in full marching order.	PBLeh
	16.8.18	9.0am	Battalion Scheme of Intensive Training resumed.	PBLeh
	17.8.18	8.30am	Training as on 16th inst.	
Ref Sheet HAZEBROUCK 5A 1/100,000	18.8.18	11am	Orders received by Vth Army over the telephone, and confirmed by written instructions received 6.30pm to place one company at disposal of 10th Brigade R.A.F. to protect aerodromes from hostile bombing machine. D Coy was detailed for this purpose and after conferring with the G.O.C. 10th Brigade R.A.F., Major Gilbert M.C. decided to dispose of his company as follows :- 1 Section at RELY Aerodrome (42 squadron R.A.F.) under Capt Higginbottom and Lieut. Goodman. 1 Section at RECLINGHEM Aerodrome under 2/Lt Pike and 2/Lt Pickles. 2 Sections at SERNY Aerodrome under Lieut Dane and 2/Lt Philbin. Coy Headquarters was to be at SERNY. This company moved off by motor lorries at 6.30 pm - no horse transport accompanied them.	PBLeh

D. D. & L., London, E.C.
(A10266) Wt W5300/P713 750,000 2/18 Sch. 52 Forms/C2118/16

Army Form C. 2118.

Instructions regarding War Diaries and Intelligence Summaries are contained in F. S. Regs., Part II. and the Staff Manual respectively. Title pages will be prepared in manuscript.

WAR DIARY
or
~~INTELLIGENCE SUMMARY.~~
(Erase heading not required.)

Place	Date	Hour	Summary of Events and Information	Remarks and references to Appendices
Ref Sheet FRANCE 36A 1/40,000 ROMBLY	19.8.18	8.30am	Battalion Training Scheme - D Coy detached for A.A. work.	PHL
	20.8.18	8.30am	Training as on 19th inst. - D Coy still away.	PHL
	21.8.18	8.30am	Training as on 19th inst. - D Coy still away.	PHL
	22.8.18	8.30am	Training as on 19th inst. - D Coy still away.	PHL
	23.8.18	8.30am	Training as on 19th inst. - D Coy still away.	PHL
	24.8.18	8.30am	Training as on 19th inst. - D Coy still away	PHL
	25.8.18	8.30am	Nothing to report - D Coy still away	PHL
	26.8.18	8.30am	Revised Scheme of Battalion Training commenced - D Coy still away	PHL
Ref. HAZEBROUCK 5a 1/100,000 and LENS 11 1/100,000. ROMBLY	27.8.18	2 am	A wire was received from 5th Army ordering the Battalion to be prepared to move on the afternoon of 27.8.18	
		9am	A wire was received from 5th Army stating that the move was to take place under orders of the 1st Army and that D Coy had been ordered to rejoin by noon on motor transport to be provided by 10th Brigade R.A.F.	
		12.20pm	Orders were received from 1st Army to move by march route to HOUDAIN and move on to GOUY SERVINS on the morning 28.8.18, coming into VIII Corps reserve, on arrival there.	PHL
		12.30pm	"D" Coy. rejoined on motor lorries and were sent on as advanced party to HOUDAIN, permission having been gained by the R.A.F. to utilize the lorries for this purpose	
HOUDAIN		2.30pm	Battalion moved off enroute for HOUDAIN, and after halting an hour for tea near BURBURE, arrived at HOUDAIN at 9.0pm. Billets in the town had been found by D Coy and were all ready.	
		11pm	Wire was received from 1st Army cancelling the move to GOUY SERVINS, and retaining the battalion in 1st Army reserve.	
	~~28.8.18~~			

D. D. & L., London, E.C.
(A10266) Wt W5300/P713 750,000 2/18 Sch. 52 Forms/C2118/16

Instructions regarding War Diaries and Intelligence Summaries are contained in F. S. Regs., Part II. and the Staff Manual respectively. Title pages will be prepared in manuscript.

WAR DIARY
or
INTELLIGENCE SUMMARY.
(Erase heading not required.)

Army Form C. 2118.

Place	Date	Hour	Summary of Events and Information	Remarks and references to Appendices
Ref. FRANCE LENS 11 1/100,000 HOUDAIN	28.8.18	11am.	Orders received from 1st Army that the battalion would move by Motor Busses to ARRAS embussing at 1st Army H.Q. and debussing at FAUBOURG ST. SAUVEUR. The transport were ordered to leave for the same destination at noon. The battalion was to be ready to move at 4.30 pm. and on arrival would come into Canadian Corps Reserve; preparations were to be made to go in the line on the evening of the 29th	
		~~3.0~~ 3.0pm	Battalion paraded in the main street of HOUDAIN and marched to the embussing point	[illegible]
Ref 51B 1/40,000 ARRAS		4.30pm	The column of busses moved off and arrived at BLANGY, the head of the column stopping at H 25 c 0.4. The battalion debussed and bivouacked ~~[illegible]~~ on the side of the road in whatever shelters or dugouts could be found; no orders were received and no preparations of any sort had been made for the arrival of the battalion. Headquarters was established in a cellar at G 29 a 0.3 – the transport made their lines at G 29 a 05.05. The C.O. reported arrival by phone to the Canadian Corps and received instructions that orders would be issued next morning.	
	29.8.18	9 am	In accordance with orders received on 28th inst all coys made preparations to go into the line in the evening; these were completed by noon.	
		11am	~~Orders were received~~ On the C.O. again reporting he received orders that the battalion would be administered by the 4th Division and was to form part of Brig-Gen Brutinel's Brigade. The C.O. was directed to report at once to Gen. Brutinel at his H.Q. which were at H 34 d 2.9.	
		~~4.30pm~~ 3.0pm	Accordingly at 3.0pm Major A.N. Richardson M.C., accompanied by the four company commanders and the signal officer reported to Gen Brutinel; at 4.30 pm Major Richardson received orders to fill up a gap which then existed between the 11th Division on the left and the 4th Division on the right.	

D. D. & L., London, E.C.
(A10266) Wt W5300/P713 750,000 2/18 Sch. 52 Forms/C2118/16

Army Form C. 2118.

WAR DIARY
or
~~INTELLIGENCE~~ SUMMARY.

(Erase heading not required.)

Instructions regarding War Diaries and Intelligence Summaries are contained in F. S. Regs., Part II. and the Staff Manual respectively. Title pages will be prepared in manuscript.

Place	Date	Hour	Summary of Events and Information	Remarks and references to Appendices
Ref Sheet FRANCE 51B 1/40,000 H 34 d 2,9	~~4.30~~ 29.8.18	4.30pm	The line to be taken up ran from O 5 d 5,8 to I 35 c 4,0 and thence was to be extended eastwards, as the 4th Division advanced. As the line eventually taken up was considered to be not in accordance with orders received, the orders are here given verbatim – "to form a defensive flank to the 11 Bde (4th British Divn) from I 35 c 4.0 to O 5 d 5,8 and thence in an E direction abreast the support elements of the left Battalion of the 11th Bde — — The 39th M.G. Bn will in addition form and hold a defensive flank from O 5 d 5,8 to P 9 central (inclusive) on the left of the 4th Divn. following the progression of the infantry."	
			On receipt of these orders OC A, B and D Coys went forward to reconnoitre the position and situation. OC C Coy. returned to ARRAS to bring up the four companies to concentrate immediately W. of ORANGE HILL. On arrival A. Coy was ordered to push forward and take up a line I 35 c 4,0 – O 5 d 5,8 with 8 Guns. D Coy were in support ~~and~~ bivouacked at H 25 a 0,2. B and C Coys returned to Arras and were disposed in shelters and dugouts in G 30 c + d.	
		9pm	The C.O. reported at HQ 11 Bde at O 7 b 6,3 and discussed the situation with the B.G.C. He found ~~that~~ the gap was even greater than had been at first supposed. Elements of the left battalion of the 11 Bde were known to be approximately holding the ground in squares O 6, I 36 and P 1. These were being withdrawn and in consequence there was probably no one in the line at the time. No knowledge had been received of the whereabouts of the enemy. Nevertheless Major Richardson, much against his own judgement, embarked on the somewhat hazardous enterprise of	

D. D. & L., London, E.C.
(A10266) Wt W5300/P713 750,000 2/18 Sch. 52 Forms/C2118/16

Instructions regarding War Diaries and Intelligence Summaries are contained in F. S. Regs., Part II. and the Staff Manual respectively. Title pages will be prepared in manuscript.

WAR DIARY
or
INTELLIGENCE SUMMARY.
(Erase heading not required.)

Army Form C. 2118.

Place	Date	Hour	Summary of Events and Information	Remarks and references to Appendices
Ref Sheet FRANCE 51B 1/40,000 O 7 b 6.3	29.8.18	9 pm	pushing unescorted Machine Guns teams into pitch blackness to fill up a gap. It was impossible to see more than a few yards ahead, the ground was unknown to every one and no touch could be gained with any infantry because of the obscurity of the situation. Orders were sent to O.C. A Coy to utilise the whole of his company in occupying a line from O 5 b 5 9 to O 6 d 8.2. D Coy were ordered up and given instructions to place 8 guns on a line from O 6 d 8.2 – P 7 b 05.95, the necessity of gaining touch with the infantry being in both cases greatly emphasised. The assistant adjutant was sent	BBLL
	30.8.18	1.20 am	for and ordered to bring up signallers and runners – he arrived at 1.20 am and found Battn H.Q. established at 11 Bde H.Q. B Coy was also ordered to concentrate W of MONCHY LE PREUX	
		3.0 am	Meanwhile in spite of overwhelming difficulties A and D Coys carried out their orders and were able to report their guns in position about 3.0 am. A Coy H.Q. was established at O 5 c 5,3 and D Coy at O 11 a 10,40. This information was at once reported by wire to Gen Brutinels H.Q	
		7.0 am	Detailed orders, together with the situation as far as known, and the probable development as far as it would affect the battalion were issued and sent out by runner. In order finally to clear up the situation Major A.N. Richardson M.C. then went forward to reconnoitre. O.C. B Coy reported his company concentrated at N 6 a central	
		11.30 am	Verbal orders were received from the G.O.C. 11 Bde that the guns on the line O 6 b – P 7 b were to advance, supported by B Coy 1st Hampshires, and make good the line GALLEY WOOD – KASHMIR WOOD. On completion of this operation B Coy was to return to its position in reserve, leaving the M.G.s unprotected. It then transpired that this	

D. D. & L., London, E.C.
(A10266) Wt W5300/P713 750,000 2/18 Sch. 52 Forms/C2118/16

Army Form C. 2118.

WAR DIARY
or
~~INTELLIGENCE~~ SUMMARY.

(Erase heading not required.)

Instructions regarding War Diaries and Intelligence Summaries are contained in F. S. Regs., Part II. and the Staff Manual respectively. Title pages will be prepared in manuscript.

Place	Date	Hour	Summary of Events and Information	Remarks and references to Appendices
Ref Sheet FRANCE 51B 1/40,000 O 7 6 6.3	30.8.18	11.30am	had been the line held by the 1st Hampshires before they withdrew on the night 29/30th of which this was the first notification received by the battalion. These orders were issued after a consultation ~~with~~ between Gen Brutinel and G.O.C. 11 Bde – and were of the utmost urgency, as the escort detailed were required by GOC 11 Bde for his attack on ETERPIGNY, which was timed to take place at 4.0pm. In the absence of Major Richardson, the assistant adjutant considered the circumstances urgent enough for him to get out operation orders for this operation on his own initiative, though the policy of pushing forward Machine Guns over open country in broad daylight without inadequate infantry protection, seemed somewhat risky.	RDh
		Noon	Accordingly orders were sent out by runner at noon for O.C A and D Coys to carry out this advance in conjunction with O.C. B Coy 1st Hampshires. Unfortunately this runner was knocked senseless by a shell and the orders were never received.	
		1.30pm	Major A.N. Richardson M.C. returned and expressed himself satisfied at the course taken by the assistant adjutant	
		3.0pm	B Coy 1st Hampshires reported their task completed, but no reports were received from either A or D Coys.	
		3.30pm	Gen. Brutinel moved his HQ. to O 7 b 6.3 and issued orders that the Battn would again move forward and make good the line P 1 d 7.9 – J 31 d 6.7 – J 31 d 1.9 – I 36 b 6.8 – I 36 a 3.8, in order to control the crossings of the COJEUL and SENSEE rivers and the LE TRINQUIS brook in squares P2, J 33, J26, and J 25.	

D. D. & L., London, E.C.
(A10266) Wt W5300/P713 750,000 2/18 Sch. 52 Forms/C2118/16

Instructions regarding War Diaries and Intelligence Summaries are contained in F. S. Regs., Part II. and the Staff Manual respectively. Title pages will be prepared in manuscript.

WAR DIARY
or
~~INTELLIGENCE SUMMARY.~~

(*Erase heading not required.*)

Army Form C. 2118.

Place	Date	Hour	Summary of Events and Information	Remarks and references to Appendices
Ref. Sheet FRANCE 51B 1/40,000	30.8.18	3.30pm	B Coy 1st Kings Own Regt. was detailed to act as escort, and the whole operation was put in charge of Major Gilbert M.C. Orders were at once sent out to O.C. A and D Coy, and the same time O.C. C Coy was ordered to concentrate his company W. of MONCHY LE PREUX	
		6.30pm	O.C. B Coy 1st Kings Own Regt was guided up and reported to Major ~~Richardson~~ Gilbert at 6.30 pm.	
		4 pm	Orders were issued from Canadian Corps that the 33rd Brigade (11th British division) would take over the front occupied by Gen Brutinel's Brigade on the right 30/31 August, and that the 39th Batt M.G.C. would be attached to the 33rd Bde. Major Richardson was shewed these orders and after consultation with the B.G.C. 33rd Bde decided to have guides to meet strong patrols of the 6th Lincolns (left Battn.) and 7th South Staffords (Right Battn.) at 8pm at O 5 c [illegible] to shew them where the line ran. Brigade H.Q. was to be established at O 8 c 2,8	
		6.30pm	These orders were transmitted to O.C. A and D Coys by the assistant adjutant, as no runners were then available.	
O 8 c 2,7		7.30pm	O.C. "C" Coy reported his coy concentrated at N 12 b 5.9. As the whole Battalion was now attached to 33rd Brigade, Major Richardson moved his H.Q. to PICK CAVES O 8 c 2.7.	
		8.0pm	The operation ordered at 3.30pm was commenced, but no reports were received up to midnight. Accordingly Major A.N. Richardson M.C. went up to forward Coys. He found that the operation was successful on the left but touch with the right guns	

D. D. & L., London, E.C. (A10266) Wt W5300/P713 750,000 2/18 Sch. 52 Forms/C2118/16

WAR DIARY
or
INTELLIGENCE SUMMARY.
(*Erase heading not required.*)

Army Form C. 2118.

Instructions regarding War Diaries and Intelligence Summaries are contained in F. S. Regs., Part II. and the Staff Manual respectively. Title pages will be prepared in manuscript.

Place	Date	Hour	Summary of Events and Information	Remarks and references to Appendices
Ref. Sheet FRANCE 51B 1/40,000	30.8.18	11.55pm	under Lt Dane in the valley had been lost. They had passed through v. heavy shelling. No reports were received from his sections until the morning; with Lt Dane, because touch had been lost, and the other because the officer Lt C.C. Shaw M.C. and his sergeant had been killed.	
			The situation became very obscure at this point, but the patrols of the 6th Lincolns and 7th South Staffords pushed forward to the line indicated, and	[initials]
Vicinity of BOIRY Notre DAME	31.8.18	1.am	succeeded in consolidating this line by 9 pm on the left and 1 am 31.8.18 on the right. Casualties during this period were 1 O.R. killed, 1 O.R. died of wounds and 7 wounded.	1 OR. Gassed
		7.0am	Reports were received of the exact situation. H.Q. of A and D Coys were established at O 5 b 5,3. Pairs of guns were in position at I 30 c 6,5 I 30 c 65,40 I 30 c 8,4 I 30 d 1,5 J 31 c 4,8 J 31 c 45,70 J 31 c 4,3 J 31 c 35,20. I 36 b 9,2 I 36 b 8,35 I 36 b 60,70 8 Guns in Reserve O 11 a 0.4.	

D. D. & L., London, E.C.
(A10266) Wt W5300/P713 750,000 2/18 Sch. 52 Forms/C2118/16

Army Form C, 2118.

Instructions regarding War Diaries and Intelligence Summaries are contained in F. S. Regs., Part II. and the Staff Manual respectively. Title pages will be prepared in manuscript.

WAR DIARY
or
INTELLIGENCE SUMMARY.
(Erase heading not required.)

Place	Date	Hour	Summary of Events and Information	Remarks and references to Appendices
Ref Sheet FRANCE 51B 1/40,000	31.8.18	7.0am	The Coy of 1st Kings Own retired, as the 6th Lincolns and 7th South Staffords had now thoroughly consolidated.	
			The day was spent in consolidation.	
		9.0pm	An order was issued by 11th Division, reorganising the Machine Guns with the Division. This was following by an Operation Order from the 11th Batt M.G.C. to the	
		11.30pm	effect that the whole 39th Battalion was now under the control of Col. Berry M.C. commandin 11th Battn M.G.C. B and A Coys were attached to 33rd Inf. Bde and were to form the Right group of the M.G.s of the division under the command of Major Gilbert M.C. C and B Coys were placed in divisional reserve.	
		11.45pm	In accordance with these orders Major Richardson ordered A Coy to take over the whole front line, and D Coy to withdraw their 8 guns in the front line into support, and form a second line of defence.	
			By morning 1.9.18 these orders were carried out, and the guns were then disposed as follows	
			A Coy – 8 Guns in I 30 c and d 8 Guns in J 31 c	
			D Coy – 8 Guns at I 36 c 5,1 O 6 a 5,7 O 6 a central O 6 a 4,1 O 6 c 4,7 O 6 c 25,50 O 11 c 5,7 O 11 a 1,35,	

D. D. & L., London, E.C.
(A10266) Wt W5300/P713 750,000 2/18 Sch. 52 Forms/C2118/16

Instructions regarding War Diaries and Intelligence Summaries are contained in F. S. Regs., Part II. and the Staff Manual respectively. Title pages will be prepared in manuscript.

WAR DIARY
or
INTELLIGENCE SUMMARY.
(Erase heading not required.)

Army Form C. 2118.

Place	Date	Hour	Summary of Events and Information	Remarks and references to Appendices
Ref Sheet FRANCE 51B 1/40,000	31.8.18	–	D Coy (cont.) 8 Guns concentrated in reserve at O 11 a 0,6. Throughout these operations great difficulty and confusion arose owing to orders emanating from different authorities – many of them were verbal, and in some cases no copies of orders were received; they were shewn for a few minutes only. In addition nearly all moves and siting of gun positions had to take place during the nights, which at this time were very dark – the country was very difficult owing to shell holes and barbed wire; the country was unknown to everyone, and in no cases could guides be obtained. Casualties during 31st inst were Lt C.C. Shaw M.C. killed 2 O.R. killed 1 O.R. wounded. A Fleetwood Wilson Lt Col. Commanding 39 Army M.G. Battalion	[initials]

D. D. & L., London, E.C.
(A10266) Wt W5300/P713 750,000 2/18 Sch. 52 Forms/C2118/16

4

CONFIDENTIAL

39th (ARMY) MACHINE GUN BATTALION.

WAR DIARY

FROM 1ST SEPT TO 30TH SEPT. 1918.

VOLUME VII

39

V.R. 7

Instructions regarding War Diaries and Intelligence Summaries are contained in F. S. Regs., Part II. and the Staff Manual respectively. Title pages will be prepared in manuscript.

WAR DIARY ~~or~~ ~~INTELLIGENCE SUMMARY.~~

(Erase heading not required.)

Army Form C. 2118.

Place	Date	Hour	Summary of Events and Information	Remarks and references to Appendices
Ref. FRANCE Sheet 51 B 1/40,000 Bn. H.Q. O 8 c 2,9.	1.9.18	Midnight.	C.O. on return from a consultation with Lt. Col Barry, issued a warning order that:– "A" Coy would be attached to 33rd Inf. Bde. and reorganise the defence of the Brigade front E. of line BOIRY-NOTRE-DAME – LADY-LANE, forming part of the right group. "D" Coy would form the other part of the right group, which was to be attached to 33rd Inf. Bde, and be under the command of Major Gilbert M.C. The guns of D Coy to be distributed in depth in defence of the same front W. of LADY LANE. Group H.Q. to be at VERT WORK. Remaining Coys to be in Divisional Reserve, remaining in their present position. Whole battalion to be under the command of Lt. Col Barry, O.C. 11th Bn. M.G.C.	
		1.0am	Telephone message was received asking the C.O. to meet Lt Col. Barry at FOSSES FM (N 12) at 7.0am.	[signature]
		2.30am	Written orders concerning reorganisation of guns were received from 11th Bn M.G.C.	
		5.0am	Orders dispatched to A and D Coys that the instructions contained in the warning order would be carried out at once. ~~#~~ Group H.Q. would be established at O 5 b 3,5 and not as previously ordered.	
		7.0am	C.O. accompanied by O.C. "B" & "C" Coys met Lt. Col. Barry at FOSSES FM. At this conference Lt. Col. Barry stated that the Canadian Corps would attack the DROCOURT-QUEANT Switch at 5.0am on the 2nd inst. The left flank (4th British Division) expected trouble from ETAING. 24 guns of the battalion were to be detailed to neutralize ETAING. For this purpose "D" Coy. and two sections of B Coy.– the whole under Major Gilbert, were detailed. ~~The a~~ Short instructions were given to O.C. B & C Coys and later to O.C. A and D Coys.	

D. D. & L., London, E.C. (A10266) Wt W5300/P713 750,000 2/18 Sch. 52 Forms/C2118/16

Army Form C. 2118.

Instructions regarding War Diaries and Intelligence Summaries are contained in F. S. Regs., Part II. and the Staff Manual respectively. Title pages will be prepared in manuscript.

WAR DIARY
~~or~~
~~INTELLIGENCE SUMMARY.~~
(Erase heading not required.)

Place	Date	Hour	Summary of Events and Information	Remarks and references to Appendices
Ref. FRANCE Sheet 51B 1/40,000 Bn.H.Q. O 8 c 2,9.	1.9.18	8.30am	Detailed orders would follow. The barrage was to neutralise the area { P 3 d 2,2 / P 3 b 2,5 / P 3 c 3,2 / P 3 a 3,5 } and last from zero to zero + 3 hours. The left of the attack was to be a line running E. and W. through P 9 c 0,8.	
		9.30am	Major Gilbert carried out his reconnaisance and sited the battery positions S. of CORNER COPSE (J 31 c 0,0.)	
		2.0pm	Capt Boyle (i/c 2 Sections "B" Coy.) reported to Major Gilbert and after consultation decided to site his guns on the right of "D" Coy. Meanwhile the 2 Sections of "B" Coy. moved forward to the vicinity of VERT WORK; these sections arrived about 3 pm, when the section officers went forward to receive orders from Capt. Boyle. Preparations for the barrage were commenced and work on the positions was started as soon as it became dusk. The battery positions were constructed as follows:- 1 and 2 Sections of "D" Coy under Lt. Dane at O 6 b 5,8. 3 and 4 Sections of "D" Coy. under Lt Goodman at O 6 b 45,40. 1 and 3 Sections of "B" Coy under Capt Boyle at O 6 b 5,0. Group H.Q. at O 5 b 3,5.	PLL
		7.0pm	Detailed orders from 11th Batt. M.G.C. were received, and orders issued to Coys at 8.30 pm. as follows:- "A" Coy. To remain silent throughout the operation and be prepared to engage and counter attack.	

D. D. & L., London, E.C.
(A10266) Wt W5300/P713 750,000 2/18 Sch. 52 Forms/C2118/16

Instructions regarding War Diaries and Intelligence Summaries are contained in F. S. Regs., Part II. and the Staff Manual respectively. Title pages will be prepared in manuscript.

WAR DIARY
or
~~INTELLIGENCE SUMMARY.~~
(Erase heading not required.)

Army Form C. 2118.

Place	Date	Hour	Summary of Events and Information	Remarks and references to Appendices
Ref. FRANCE Sheet 51B 1/40,000. Bn. H.Q. O 8 c 2.9.	1.9.18	8.30pm	"B" Coy. to move forward with transport, and at zero to be prepared to reinforce, if necessary. The 2 Sections engaged on barrage to rejoin the Coy at Zero + 3 hours. ("B" Coy (less two sections) arrived at VERT WORK at 1.5 am.) "C" Coy. to be prepared to move forward at Zero. "D" Coy. to resume defensive positions previously held by them at zero + 3 hours, except that the 2 sections which would normally be held in reserve would take up positions in P 1 a in order to engage any enemy seen retiring through J 33 a + c. These guns would not be withdrawn until further orders. All preparations (including the linking up of batteries to Group H.Q. by telephone) were completed by 11.0pm. Casualties – 1 O.R. died of wounds.	[initials]
	2.9.18	5am – 8am	Steady barrage was maintained on ETAING, 120,000 rounds being fired. The attack was completely successful. Prisoners stated that it was impossible to emerge from dugouts in ETAING owing to M.G. fire.	
		8.0am	Barrage positions were abandoned and fresh dispositions taken up as ordered. These were completed by 9.30 am. No counter attack developed and no further firing ~~was~~ was done during the day.	[initials]
		1.0pm	O.C. "C" Coy moved to Bn. H.Q. in order to maintain closer touch with the situation. Casualties – 1 O.R. wounded.	

D. D. & L., London, E.C.
(A10266) Wt W5300/P713 750,000 2/18 Sch. 52 Forms/C2118/16

Army Form C. 2118.

WAR DIARY
or
INTELLIGENCE SUMMARY.
(Erase heading not required.)

Instructions regarding War Diaries and Intelligence Summaries are contained in F. S. Regs., Part II. and the Staff Manual respectively. Title pages will be prepared in manuscript.

Place	Date	Hour	Summary of Events and Information	Remarks and references to Appendices
Ref. FRANCE Sheet 51B 1/40.000 Bn.H.Q.-O.8.c.2.9.	3.9.18	1.0pm.	After consultation with A Col: Barry, the C.O. issued orders for:- "B" Coy. to deploy 2 sections (i) to cover valley S. of BOIRY firing S.E. (ii) to cover ridge E. of BOIS DU SART firing N.E. "D" Coy to withdraw the 8 guns in P 1 a and take up positions W. of LADY LANE to cover (i) LONG VALLEY (ii) Ridge E. of BOIRY. Orders were also issued for the following reliefs to take place, the new dispositions being handed over when they had been completed; the whole to take place on the night 3/4th. "C" Coy to relieve "A" Coy. in the front Line "B" Coy to relieve "D" Coy. in support. Relieved Coys to take over duties of Coys by which they had been relieved. "B" Coy transport to return to vicinity of MONCHY LE PREUX Right Group (B + C Coys) to be commanded by Major Platts M.C. New dispositions and all reliefs were completed in accordance with these orders by midnight. Casualties 4 O.R. killed 1 O.R. died of wounds. 3 O.R. wounded	[initials]

D. D. & L., London, E.C.
(A10266) Wt W5300/P713 750,000 2/18 Sch. 52 Forms/C2118/16

Army Form C. 2118.

WAR DIARY
or
~~INTELLIGENCE SUMMARY.~~
(Erase heading not required.)

Instructions regarding War Diaries and Intelligence Summaries are contained in F. S. Regs., Part II. and the Staff Manual respectively. Title pages will be prepared in manuscript.

Place	Date	Hour	Summary of Events and Information	Remarks and references to Appendices
Ref. FRANCE Sheet 51B 1/40,000	4.9.18	MIDNIGHT	Situation was as follows:-	
			"A" Coy (with transport) concentrated W of MONCHY at N 6 central	
			"B" Coy. in support positions south and east of BOIRY in squares O 5, 6, & 11 forming Part of right group, with H.Q. at O 5 c 3,5.	
Bn H.Q. O 8 c 2,9.			"C" Coy in front Line in positions in squares I 30 and 36, and J 31, forming part of right group, with H.Q. at O 5 c 3,5.	
			"D" Coy. concentrated at VERT WORK, with one section in position in O 3 and one section in position at O 9.	PBLL
			Transport Lines of B, C, and D Coys, W of MONCHY at O 2 c	
			Batt. H.Q in PICK CAVES O 8 c 2,9.	
			Rear H.Q. at G 30 d 0,4.	
			The day passed quietly; after dusk two guns were moved ~~f~~ forward from J 31 to J 32 c to support the infantry outpost line.	
			Casualties 1 O.R. wounded	
	5.9.18	-	Trench Routine. Positions were generally consolidated, and further dumps of S.A.A. were formed - 50 Boxes at D Coy H.Q.	
			100 Boxes at CORNER COPSE J 31 c 0,0.	PBLL
			Casualties 2 O.R. wounded 1 O.R. gassed	

D. D. & L., London, E.C.
(A10266) Wt W5300/P713 750,000 2/18 Sch. 52 Forms/C2118/16

Army Form C. 2118.

Instructions regarding War Diaries and Intelligence Summaries are contained in F. S. Regs., Part II. and the Staff Manual respectively. Title pages will be prepared in manuscript.

WAR DIARY
or
INTELLIGENCE SUMMARY.
(Erase heading not required.)

Place	Date	Hour	Summary of Events and Information	Remarks and references to Appendices
Ref. FRANCE Sheet 51B 1/40,000	6.9.18		Trench Routine	
		1.0pm	Lt Col Fleetwood Wilson returned and resumed command of the battalion.	
Bn H.Q. 08c2.9		3.0pm	Batt H.Q. moved from PICK CAVES and was established at G 30 d 0,4.	
Bn H.Q. G30d0,4		8.0pm	Orders were issued by 11 Division that the 32nd Inf Bde would take over the whole of the divisional front on the night 7/8th; the 39th Army M.G. Battalion would be withdrawn to the FEUCHY area. Casualties – NIL.	
	7.9.18	10.0am	Orders by 11th Batt. M.G.C. were received that "C" and "D" Coys 11th Batt M.G.C. would relieve the right group under Major Platts M.C.	
		11.0am	Orders were issued in accordance with the orders received from 11th Division + 11th Bn MGC "A" Coy to withdraw to the vicinity of G 30 d 0,4. "B" Coy to hand over 12 Gun positions to portions of "C" + "D" Coys 11th Batt M.G.C. "C" Coy to hand over 8 Gun positions to portions of "D" Coy 11th Batt. M.G.C. "D" Coy to be relieved by "C" Coy 11th Batt M.G.C. Arrangements to be made by O.C.s concerned. All guns not relieved to be withdrawn. After relief all Coys to concentrate in the vicinity of G 30 d 0,4.	
	8.9.18	2.30am	The above reliefs were duly carried out and the whole battalion including transport were concentrated in the vicinity of G 30 d by 2.30 am 8.9.18 where the troops were disposed such dugouts and shelters as were available. Casualties – 1 O.R. wounded and remained at duty	

D. D. & L., London, E.C.
(A10256) Wt W5300/P713 750,000 2/18 Sch. 52 Forms/C2118/16

Instructions regarding War Diaries and Intelligence Summaries are contained in F. S. Regs., Part II. and the Staff Manual respectively. Title pages will be prepared in manuscript.

WAR DIARY

or

~~INTELLIGENCE SUMMARY.~~

(Erase heading not required.)

Army Form C. 2118.

Place	Date	Hour	Summary of Events and Information	Remarks and references to Appendices
Ref. FRANCE Sheet 51 B 1/40,000	8.9.18		Reorganisation carried out by all companies.	
		11.10pm	At 11.10pm. orders were received by wire from XXII Corps for the battalion to move to GAUCHIN-LE-GAL at 2 pm 9.9.18. and be prepared to move on next day to Another Army.	R.B.L.
G 30 d 0,4 LENS 11 1/100,000	9.9.18	2.0pm	Battalion left by march route for GAUCHIN-LE-GAL and arrived at 9.0pm. thus coming into 1st Army reserve. The Battalion billetted here for the night.	
		10.30pm	Orders received from 1st Army to move by march route to LIERES 10.9.18.	R.B.L.
GAUCHIN-LE-GAL (H 2. 00, 95)	10.9.18	11.0am	Battalion left by march route for LIERES and arrived at 5.0pm coming into 5th Army reserve; billets were obtained here for the night.	
HAZEBROUCK 5a 1/100,000 LIERES (F 6. 65, 60.		8.30pm	Orders received from XV Corps that the battalion was transferred to 2nd Army and had been allotted to the XV Corps. The Battalion was to be attached to the 40th Division and was to move to MORBECQUE at 9.30 am. 11.9.18; on arrival the Battalion was to go into the line and relieve the 104 Batt. M.G.C.	
		9.0pm	Detailed orders concerning above relief arrived from 40th Division. 12.9.18. One Coy. in reserve near LE VERRIER (I 4 72, 40) to be relieved. 13.9.18. One Coy. in advanced guard to be relieved by the Battalion's Coy in reserve. The Coy. relieved to go into reserve. Two Coys in main line of resistance to be relieved. 14.9.18. One Coy. in reserve to be relieved. Bn H.Q. to be relieved and command of the M.G. defence to pass to the Battalion.	R.B.L.

D. D. & L., London, E.C.
(A10266) Wt W5300/P713 750,000 2/18 Sch. 52 Forms/C2118/16

Army Form C. 2118.

Instructions regarding War Diaries and Intelligence Summaries are contained in F. S. Regs., Part II. and the Staff Manual respectively. Title pages will be prepared in manuscript.

WAR DIARY
or
~~INTELLIGENCE SUMMARY.~~

(Erase heading not required.)

Place	Date	Hour	Summary of Events and Information	Remarks and references to Appendices
Ref FRANCE Sheet HAZEBROUCK 5A 1/100,000	11·9·18	9·30am	Battalion left by march route for MORBECQUE and arrived 3·30pm. The C.O. reported to 40th Division and asked if it were possible to postpone the relief by one day. This request was granted	[signature]
LIERES MORBECQUE	12·9·18	10·0am	Reorganisation and preparation for the line. Coy. commanders reconnoitred the positions to be taken over.	[signature]
~~13·9·18~~				
36A NE } 36 NW } 1/20,000	13·9·18	9·30am	"B" Coy. moved off on lorries provided by 104 Batt. M.G.C. to relieve the reserve Coy. which was concentrated in the vicinity of DU BOIS FARM (A 19 b 6,5). At LABIS FM (F 13 central) they debussed and moved by march route to DU BOIS FARM. Relief was complete at 4 p.m	[signature]
	14·9·18	8·30am	"C" Coy moved off by lorries provided by 104 Batt. M.G.C. to relieve right Coy. in Main Line of Resistance. H.Q. at WHIST HOUSE A 20 c 9.3. Guides were met at LABIS FM. whence the Coy proceeded by march route. Relief was complete at 5·45 pm.	
		10·0am	"D" Coy. following the same procedure relieved the right Coy. in the Main Line of Resistance. H.Q. at A 15 d 75,75 - OSPREY HOUSE. Relief was complete at 5·40 pm.	[signature]
		5pm	"B" Coy. moved forward from reserve coy. by march route to relieve Coy. in outpost line. Relief was complete at 11·0pm. The same H.Q. was not taken over, but was established at A 30 a 3.0. The relieved Coy. concentrated and became Reserve Coy.	
	15·9·18	9·0am	"A" Coy. following the same procedure as "B" Coy on the 13th inst. moved off to relieve the Reserve Coy - Relief was complete at 3·45 pm. In the meantime the signal communication had been taken over and altered. All Coys were connected up by direct lines to the Battalion Exchange	[signature]

D. D. & L., London, E.C.
(A10266) Wt W5300/P713 750,000 2/18 Sch. 52 Forms/C2118/16

Army Form C. 2118.

Instructions regarding War Diaries and Intelligence Summaries are contained in F. S. Regs., Part II. and the Staff Manual respectively. Title pages will be prepared in manuscript.

WAR DIARY
~~or~~
~~INTELLIGENCE SUMMARY.~~
(Erase heading not required.)

Place	Date	Hour	Summary of Events and Information	Remarks and references to Appendices
Ref FRANCE 36ANE / 36NW 1/20,000 MORBECQUE F24a 2,7	15.9.18	1.0pm	Bn. H.Q. moved off in lorries from 40 Division to take over Batt H.Q. at F24 a 2,7 Relief was complete for the whole Battalion at 4.0pm.	
			The situation was this.	
			B Coy in outpost line, with main line of resistance running through B16, B.22, B.28, B27, B26, H1. H.Q. A 30 a 3,0.	
			D Coy on left of Divisional main line of resistance, disposed in depth in squares A 16, 17, 18, 22, 23, 24. H.Q. A 15 d 75,75	RSLL
			C Coy on right of Divisional main line of resistance, disposed in squares A 27, 29, G 2, 3 and 5. H.Q. A 20 c 9,3	
			(Divisional Line runs through A 17, 23, 29, G 4, 10.	
			A Coy concentrated in vicinity A 19 b 6,5.	
			Orders Divisional Line to be held at all costs.	
	16.9.18		Trench Routine - Sector Quiet.	
		8.30pm	Orders received from Division, changing whole defence scheme.	
			One Brigade was to be in front system, holding the line	RSLL
			One Brigade in support, disposed West of STEENWERCK and ready to move at 1 hours notice.	
			One Brigade in rest in the HAZEBROUCK Area, ready to move at 2½ hours notice	

D. D. & L., London, E.C.
(A10266) Wt W5300/P713 750,000 2/18 Sch. 52 Forms/C2118/16

Army Form C. 2118.

WAR DIARY
or
~~INTELLIGENCE SUMMARY.~~
(Erase heading not required.)

Instructions regarding War Diaries and Intelligence Summaries are contained in F. S. Regs., Part II. and the Staff Manual respectively. Title pages will be prepared in manuscript.

Place	Date	Hour	Summary of Events and Information	Remarks and references to Appendices
Ref FRANCE Sheet 36 NW / 36a NE 1/20,000	16·9·18		The main line of resistance was to be the NIEPPE system running through squares B 16, 22, 27, 26. This line would be reinforced by the support Brigade if necessary. The Battalion to have one Coy. with the forward Brigade, and another Coy in position to cover the guns and form a belt of fire from B 16 d to JESUS FARM (B 26 d.) One Coy to remain in reserve as before, and one coy to be in rest at HAZEBROUCK.	[illegible initials]
	17·9·18	4 pm	Accordingly orders were issued for the following reorganisation to take place on the 18th inst:- C Coy to relieve B in the front system; D Coy to take over defence of the artillery; B Coy to withdraw to HAZEBROUCK; A Coy to remain in reserve.	[illegible initials]
			Trench routine - more active. Casualties 1 O.R. wounded.	
	18·9·18		After reconnaisance reliefs took place in accordance with orders issued 17·9·18.	
		2 pm	D Coy moved forward to positions sited to defend artillery, and completed their dispositions by 4.50 pm. H.Q. remained unchanged.	
		6·0 pm	C Coy moved forward to relieve "B" Coy. - Relief was complete at 10.5 pm. B Coy on relief were conveyed by lorries to HAZEBROUCK, arriving at 3 am. They were billetted in houses in the vicinity of D 3 b 2,7. (H.Q.) Casualties 3 O.R. wounded	[illegible initials]

Army Form C. 2118.

Instructions regarding War Diaries and Intelligence Summaries are contained in F. S. Regs., Part II. and the Staff Manual respectively. Title pages will be prepared in manuscript.

WAR DIARY
or
~~INTELLIGENCE SUMMARY.~~

(Erase heading not required.)

Place	Date	Hour	Summary of Events and Information	Remarks and references to Appendices
Ref. FRANCE Sheet 36 NW 36A NE 1/20,000. F 24 a 10.75	19.9.18	–	Trench Routine. Reinforcements arrived – Lt J.R. Barr, 2/Lt W.G. Perkins, 11 O.R.s	[signature]
	20.9.18	–	Trench Routine. Sector quieter than at first.	[signature]
	21.9.18	–	Trench Routine.	
		11.0pm	Orders issued from 40th Division that the front of the Division would be extend to the North and the Divl. Boundary run C 1 b 1.0 – B 5 c 0.2 – B 12 a 0.0 thence as before. This frontage was to be taken over by the Brigade in rest (119 Inf. Bde) and 1 Coy. from the battalion on the night 23/24 Sept. from the 31st Divn.	[signature]
			Casualties 1 OR Killed. 1 O.R. Wounded. 1 O.R. Gassed.	
	22.9.18	–	Trench Routine.	
		8.30pm	Orders issued by battalion in accordance with orders received from 40th Division. "A" Coy. to be attached to 119 Inf. Bde; to take over 8 guns from 31st Bn M.G.C. and dispose of the remainder as ordered by G.O.C. 119 Inf Bde. "B" Coy. to move forward and relieve "A" Coy. on the 23rd inst, by rail to BAILLEUL, thence by march route. A Coy to be prepared to move forward and relieve on the night 23/24th. Casualties – nil	[signature]

D. D. & L., London, E.C.
(A10266) Wt W5300/P713 750,000 2/18 Sch. 52 Forms/C2118/16

Instructions regarding War Diaries and Intelligence Summaries are contained in F. S. Regs., Part II. and the Staff Manual respectively. Title pages will be prepared in manuscript.

WAR DIARY
or
~~INTELLIGENCE SUMMARY.~~

(Erase heading not required.)

Army Form C. 2118.

Place	Date	Hour	Summary of Events and Information	Remarks and references to Appendices
Ref. FRANCE Sheet 36 NW 36A NE 1/20,000 Bn. H.Q. F 24 a 10,75.	22.9.18	10 pm	Orders issued by 40 Division that on early morning of 24th inst. the 121st Inf. Bde would advance and capture the line of L.ps from ~~present~~ B 22 d 9.9 to B 18 d 1,8, thence to B 18 a 0.5 – B 12 c 2,0 – thence to present line at OOSTHOVE FM. A line of patrols would be pushed out 600 yards in advance of this and make good the line C 13 c 2,8 – C 7 c 2,3 thence to original line at B 12 b 0,6. This operation to be referred to as sawdust. An M.G. enfilade barrage was to be put down in part of the artillery barrage from the vicinity of B 5. This was to be the work of the Battalion.	[illegible]
	23.9.18		Trench Routine	
		MIDDAY	Extension of front was postponed indefinitely.	
		2.0pm	SAWDUST was postponed 48 hours, and the 31st Battn M.G.C. asked to provide the M.G. barrage, as the Battalion would not now be moving to the left.	
		6.30pm	Orders issued by Battalion for "B" Coy. to relieve "C" Coy. in front line on night 24/25th; on relief "C" Coy. to proceed to WHIST HOUSE (A 20 c 8,1) and be disposed in shelters in the vicinity.	[illegible]
	24.9.18		Trench Routine.	
		3.0pm	After consultation with the acting G.S.O. I the C.O. obtained permission for "A" Coy. to carry out the relief ordered 22.9.18 on the night 25/26th. It was understood that SAWDUST had been further postponed and would be carried out at dawn on 27th. 31st BATT. M.G.C. would therefore be relieved of the task of providing an enfilade M.G. barrage in support of this operation. "A" Coy. was now detailed to carry this out. Casualties - Lt. Goodman, 2/Lt. Clayton } sick.	[illegible]

D. D. & L., London, E.C.
(A10266) Wt W5300/P713 750,000 2/18 Sch. 52 Forms/C2118/16

Army Form C. 2118.

WAR DIARY
or
~~INTELLIGENCE SUMMARY.~~

(*Erase heading not required.*)

Instructions regarding War Diaries and Intelligence Summaries are contained in F. S. Regs., Part II. and the Staff Manual respectively. Title pages will be prepared in manuscript.

Place	Date	Hour	Summary of Events and Information	Remarks and references to Appendices
Ref. FRANCE Sheet. 36 NW 36A NE 1/20,000. Bn H.Q. F24a10.75	24.9.18	11 pm	Orders issued for "A" Coy. to carry out relief, as ordered 22.9.18, on night 25/26th.	
	25.9.18		Trench Routine.	
		11.45am	Orders were issued by 40th Division that the extension of front ordered 21.9.18 would take place on night 26/27th inst.	
		6.30pm	40th Division issued orders that SAWDUST would take place on the morning of 27th inst.	[initials]
		9.22pm	"A" Coy. reported relief complete. This Coy. had now - 8 Guns in the line 4 Guns at Coy. H.Q. 4 Guns in rest at DU BOIS FM.	
	26.9.18		Trench Routine "A" Coy made preparations for the barrage in support of the attack on the 27th: this was to be carried out by 8 reserve guns **4.0pm.** Zero hour (5.30am 27th) sent to companies 6.30pm. Orders issued for 8 barrage guns of 'A' Coy to move forward on night 27/28 to B.6. central, to be prepared to assist attack by left flank division on 29th. Their role was to establish an S.O.S. barrage from C.2.a.0.0. to C.3.a.0.3 protecting the R. flank of the left Division Casualties 2 OR wded	[initials]
	27.9.18		At zero hour (5.45 am) 'A' Coy fired barrage to assist operation "SAWDUST No. of rounds fired: 23,500. 3.0pm. Orders issued cancelling Orders issued 6.30 pm 26th.	[initials]

D. D. & L., London, E.C.
(A10266) Wt W5300/P713 750,000 2/18 Sch. 52 Forms/C2118/16

Instructions regarding War Diaries and Intelligence Summaries are contained in F. S. Regs., Part II. and the Staff Manual respectively. Title pages will be prepared in manuscript.

WAR DIARY
or
~~INTELLIGENCE SUMMARY.~~
(Erase heading not required.)

Army Form C. 2118.

Place	Date	Hour	Summary of Events and Information	Remarks and references to Appendices
FRANCE Sheet 36 N.W. 36A NE 1/20000	28th		Trench Routine Reinforcements 1 OR. Casualties Lt JRBARR + 3 OR. wded	GMM
Bn. H.Q. F.24.a.10.75	29th		-Do- B. Coy. H.Q. to A.23.B.1.8 do Reo. Section B.28.B.2.7 12.0 noon Proposed scheme of defence submitted to G.O.C. 40 DIV. Reinforcements 6 O.R.	GMM
	30th		Trench Routine 3.30pm Orders for relief of B Coy by C Coy issued, together with instructions for regrouping of guns on withdrawal of 12 guns of D Coy. On rearrangement + relief by night 1/2nd guns will be disposed:	

'A' Coy.

2 guns in Reserve B8.c.1.8
H1. B9c 35.97
H2. B9c.4.7
H3. B10c.1.0
H4. B10c 2.6
F1. B5a 9.2
F2. B5a 7.1
S.H.Q. B5a. 3.2.
G1. B11a. 2.2.
G2. B11c 05.80
G3 B17a.0.7
G4. B17a.0.5
S.H.Q B12.b.5.6.

1 gun C7b.8.2
1 " C13a 3.6.
S.H.Q B12b.5.6.
2 guns B6.d.

'B' Coy.

A1 - B20.c.5.5.
A2 - B20d.95.90
A3 - B21a.0.9.
A4 - B15c 30.05.
B1 - B26.b.2.6
B2 - B21c.4.0
B3 - B21a.8.8.
B4 - B27b.1.6.
C1 - B21.d.8.5
C2 - B22.c.0.5.

C3 - B22a.6.6.
C4 - B22a 65.80
D1 - B27c.7.2
D2 - B27d.0.1
D3 - B28.c.4.8.
D4 - B28.d.8.6
E1 - H4.a.50.98.
E2 - B28d.8.6
E3 - B28b.9.1
E4 - B29a.2.6.

Lieut H.H. STURT to UK for instructional staff course M.G.T.C. — GMM

H. Hutson [signature]
Lieut. Col.
Cmdg. 39th (Army) Machine Gun Battalion.

D. D. & L., London, E.C.
(A10266) Wt W5300/P713 750,000 2/18 Sch. 52 Forms/C2118/16

CONFIDENTIAL.

WAR DIARY

of

39th (ARMY) MACHINE GUN BATTALION.

From 1st October 1918 To 31st October 1918.

VOLUME VIII.

Army Form C. 2118.

Instructions regarding War Diaries and Intelligence Summaries are contained in F. S. Regs., Part II. and the Staff Manual respectively. Title pages will be prepared in manuscript.

WAR DIARY
or
INTELLIGENCE SUMMARY.

(Erase heading not required.)

Place	Date	Hour	Summary of Events and Information	Remarks and references to Appendices

D. D. & L., London, E.C.
(A10266) Wt W5300/P713 750,000 2/18 Sch. 52 Forms/C2118/16

234

Instructions regarding War Diaries and Intelligence Summaries are contained in F. S. Regs., Part II. and the Staff Manual respectively. Title pages will be prepared in manuscript.

WAR DIARY
or
~~INTELLIGENCE SUMMARY~~.
(Erase heading not required.)

Army Form C. 2118.

Place	Date	Hour	Summary of Events and Information	Remarks and references to Appendices
FRANCE	1		Reorganization of guns continued	
Sheets 36 N.W + 36 A.NE		22.00	Relief of 'B' Coy by 'C' Coy completed. Dispositions as indicated in entry on Sept. 30th (vide. Vol. 11)	AW.
Batt. HQ. F.24.a.10.75		22.00	A Coy moved 2 guns from reserve to C.16.a.3.5	
			C. Coy HQ:- rear, B.8c.10.85 ; Adv. B.16.B.5.6	
	2.	14.45	A Coy notified change of HQ. Advanced HQ. becoming Rear HQ. Adv. HQ. moved to B.16.B.50.60	
		15.00	Dispositions of A Coy: 2 guns B.16.b.95.20	
			- do B.11.c.00.90	
			- do B.5.c.80.40	
			- do B.5.c.90.40	
			- do B.10.c.50.50	
			- do B.9.c.40.70	
			- do B.11.d.70.70	
			1 do C.7.b.70.10	
			- do C.13.a.40.50	
			Reinforcements 3 officers { 2Lt Burns F.J. - Jarvis S.L. - Anketell G.	AW.

D. D. & L., London, E.C.
(A10266) Wt W5300/P713 750,000 2/18 Sch. 52 Forms/C2118/16

Army Form C. 2118.

Instructions regarding War Diaries and Intelligence Summaries are contained in F. S. Regs., Part II. and the Staff Manual respectively. Title pages will be prepared in manuscript.

WAR DIARY
or
~~INTELLIGENCE~~ SUMMARY.

(*Erase heading not required.*)

Place	Date	Hour	Summary of Events and Information	Remarks and references to Appendices
FRANCE Sheets 36NW 36A.NE Battn. HQ F.24.A.10.75	2.	16.30	Commanding Officer attended conference at 40th (Bn.) Div. HQ. in reference to proposed advance of the division.	AW.
		21.30	40th Div. Order no. 26 received: Enemy reported withdrawing rapidly and believed going back to line of the DEULE Canal W. of LILLE. All divisions to follow up the enemy harassing him and impeding his retirement. 40th Division to work round N. + S. of ARMENTIERES as under:	
			119th Inf. Bde :- work round N. of ARMENTIERES and clear up situation E. of the town as far South as ARMENTIERES - LILLE railway	
			120th do :- take over such portion of line as held by 61st Div. N. of Divisional boundary, work round S. of ARMENTIERES keeping S. of ARMENTIERES - LILLE railway. When the advance reaches point were this railway cuts Divl boundary the bde. will become squeezed out and remain in support on right rear of Divl sector	
			Divisional Boundaries N. Grid line from C.16 central to C.18 central + eastwards	
			S. Grid line from H.10. central - H.12 central I.8 central + eastwards	AW.

D. D. & L., London, E.C. (A10266) Wt W5300/P713 750,000 2/18 Sch. 52 Forms/C2118/16

Army Form C. 2118.

WAR DIARY
or
~~INTELLIGENCE SUMMARY~~.

(Erase heading not required.)

Instructions regarding War Diaries and Intelligence Summaries are contained in F. S. Regs., Part II. and the Staff Manual respectively. Title pages will be prepared in manuscript.

Place	Date	Hour	Summary of Events and Information	Remarks and references to Appendices
FRANCE Sheet 36 N.W 36.A.NE	2	21.30	(Continuation of 40. Div. Order no. 216)	
			M.G. Companies attached to forward Bdes. to accompany these Bdes. -	
			A Coy with 119 Inf. Bde and C Coy with 120. Inf. Bde	
Batt HQ. F.24.A.10.75		22.00	Orders issued for Batt. HQ. to move forward at 10.0 a.m. 3rd to A.23.B.1.9	
	3.	09.00	66th Div. Art. Order no. 65 received: 330 Bde R.F.A to support 119 Inf. Bde; 331 do do 120 do	GM.
Batt HQ		10.00	Batt. HQ. to A.23.B.1.9	
F.24.A.10.75 to A.23.B.1.9		10.15	Information received from 'A' Coy that six rear guns were moving forward to C14	
		16.03	A Coy notified following move of guns to take effect during the night:-	
			Six guns in old British front line - C23.A.0.3 to I.5.A.7.0	
			Two do support, C.22.A.70.50 to C.28.A.70.50	
			Coy. HQ. to LE BIZET C13.B. central	
		16.30	C. Coy HQ. established at B.21.B.3.7	

CWS

D. D. & L., London, E.C.
(A10266) Wt W5300/P713 750,000 2/18 Sch. 52 Forms/C2118/16

Army Form C. 2118.

WAR DIARY
or
~~INTELLIGENCE SUMMARY.~~
(Erase heading not required.)

Instructions regarding War Diaries and Intelligence Summaries are contained in F. S. Regs., Part II. and the Staff Manual respectively. Title pages will be prepared in manuscript.

Place	Date	Hour	Summary of Events and Information	Remarks and references to Appendices
FRANCE Sheet 36 N.W 36A N.E Batt. H.Q. A.23.B.1.9	3.	17.00	40th Division wire no. G.C. 443 timed 15.57 received. Left Bde. reported 14.10 moving into old British line, Rt. Bde at 10.30 were occupying trenches in I 9.B.	
		19.30	"A" Coy. H.Q. at C.13.d.40.85	
		21.00	"C" Coy dispositions reported to be:- Coy. H.Q. B.21.B.3.7 Four guns H.5. central to H.11.B Two ~~do~~ do (Coh) H.3, B.28, Railway B.21.C., B.22.A One do (Coh) B.23, Laundry B.29, H.4.A (covering crossings of LYS) One in PENGE VILLA to B.21.C. One in B.27.B Remainder in reserve	
		23.32	40th Division wire no. G.C. 449 timed 22.55 received: Division on left report line: Trenches C.16.B, ~~C~~ 10. central, CEDILLA trench, C5, C4, C7, along railway then as before	[signature]

PUBLIC RECORD
OFFICE

Instructions regarding War Diaries and Intelligence Summaries are contained in F. S. Regs., Part II. and the Staff Manual respectively. Title pages will be prepared in manuscript.

WAR DIARY
or
INTELLIGENCE SUMMARY.
(Erase heading not required.)

Army Form C. 2118.

Place	Date	Hour	Summary of Events and Information	Remarks and references to Appendices
FRANCE Sheet 36 N.W 36.A.NE Batt. HQ A.23.B.1.9.	4.	10.00	C Coy dispositions at 08.30 received:-	
			Eight guns covering crossings { H.3.a.2.4, H.3.a.7.4, B.28.c.7.2, B.28.d.7.6, B.28.b.9.0, B.29.c.4.0, B.23.c.6.2, B.23.c.9.3	
			2 guns at B.22.a.7.5; one each at B.21.d.7.4, B.21.d.9.6, B.26.b.0.5, B.27.b.2.4, B.21.c.4.0, B.21.c.7.7, H.5.d and H.11.b.	
			Coy. HQ. B.15.d.85.60	
			C Coy reports also 4 guns attached from B Coy no longer required	
		10.15	C Coy instructed to order 4 guns 'B' Coy to rejoin their company	
		16.30	4 guns of 'B' Coy attached to 'C' Coy rejoined 'B' Coy (in reserve at STEENWERCKE	
	4/5		"A" Coy carried out inter-section relief.	AM

D. D. & L., London, E.C.
(A10266) Wt W5300/P713 750,000 2/18 Sch. 52 Forms/C2118/16

Army Form C. 2118.

WAR DIARY
or
~~INTELLIGENCE SUMMARY~~.
(Erase heading not required.)

Instructions regarding War Diaries and Intelligence Summaries are contained in F. S. Regs., Part II. and the Staff Manual respectively. Title pages will be prepared in manuscript.

Place	Date	Hour	Summary of Events and Information	Remarks and references to Appendices
FRANCE 36 N.W. 36 A. NE Batt. HQ. A.23.B.19.	4th		Trench routine, and consolidation of new positions	
		12.40	D Company (in reserve) HQ. to A.30.B.30.95	CWM
	5th	?	2 guns of C Coy at H.5.d.4.1 moved to I.2. central to engage hostile M.G. at I.3.d. Hostile gun withdrew to I.10.d and ceased activity	
		09.30	Dispositions of 'C' Coy, Coy H.Q. B.15.D.4.0	
			Section HQ. B.26 b.0.5, Guns:- { H.3.A.20.40, H.3.A.75.45 / H.3.B.9.5, B.28.C.7.2 }	
			Section HQ. B.28.b.20.65 do { B.28.D.9.9, B.29.C.5.9 / B.23.c.6.2, B.23.C.9.4 }	
			-do- B.15.d.4.0 do { B.21.d.1.0, B.21.d.85.60 / B.16.d.8.2, B.22.b.6.9 }	
			-do- H.5.D.4.1 { 2 at I.2.C / 2 at H.5.D.4.1 }	CWM

D. D. & L., London, E.C.
(A10266) Wt W5300/P713 750,000 2/18 Sch. 52 Forms/C2118/16

Army Form C. 2118.

Instructions regarding War Diaries and Intelligence Summaries are contained in F. S. Regs., Part II. and the Staff Manual respectively. Title pages will be prepared in manuscript.

WAR DIARY
or
~~INTELLIGENCE SUMMARY.~~
(Erase heading not required.)

Place	Date	Hour	Summary of Events and Information	Remarks and references to Appendices
FRANCE 36 N.W 36A N.E Batt HQ A.23.B.1.9	5	14.00	40th Division Order no. 6 received, time of issue not stated 120th Bde to relieve 119th Bde day & night of 6th and operate as advanced Guard 119th Bde to withdraw to support in NIEPPE system one company to be attached to each Bde. for M.G. Defence.	
		1600	Order no. 64 issued in accordance with 40th Div. Order no. 6. B Coy. to relieve C Coy. & operate with 119th Bde relief to take place during day of 6th & night 6th/7th C Coy. on relief to concentrate in NIEPPE, & on night 7/8th to relieve "A" Coy and operate with 120th Bde.	
		18.30	Order issued for 4 guns of "C" forward of LYS not to be relieved by B Coy but to remain manned by "C" Coy until relief of 'A' Coy on 7th	AM
	6th	05.30	Heavy enemy bombardment of front system. No attack developed	
		08.45 13.15 15.00	Hostile low flying aircraft reconnoitred NIEPPE, STEENWERCKE area and were closely engaged by A.A. guns of battalion	
		20.30	Relief of "C" Coy by B Coy complete. C Coy concentrated in NIEPPE B Coy { Adv. HQ. B.20.B.40.45 { Rear HQ. B.19.a.00.50	AM

Instructions regarding War Diaries and Intelligence Summaries are contained in F. S. Regs., Part II. and the Staff Manual respectively. Title pages will be prepared in manuscript.

WAR DIARY
or
~~INTELLIGENCE SUMMARY.~~
(Erase heading not required.)

Army Form C. 2118.

Place	Date	Hour	Summary of Events and Information	Remarks and references to Appendices
FRANCE 36.N.W 36A.N.E.	7th	12.15	Relief orders of "A" Coy (O.O. 31) timed 11.00 received	
		2152	Relief of "A" Coy by "C" Coy complete 21.52	AW
Batt HQ A.23.B.1.9	8th	0900	Dispositions of C Coy:	
			Coy HQ. I.1.D.65.50	
			Section HQ (4 guns) C 22.C.2.6 { Guns at C.28.a.7.3, C.22.C.75.45 / do C.22.C.3.5, C.22.a.8.6	
			do (2 guns) I.3.d.77 { do I 4.d.3.1 / I.4.A.9.5	
			do (2 guns) C.28.A.4.1 { do C.28.A.1.1 / C.28.A.7.0	
			do (4 guns) C.14.D.20.25 { do C.21.C.1.7, C.21.C.1.8 / C.15.D.25.95, C.15.d.35.90	
			do H.6.D.65.50 4 guns in I.7. covering artillery	
			Dispositions of B Coy	
			Coy HQ. B.20.B.40.45 Rear HQ. B.19.A.0.5	
			Guns as on relief of C Coy 6/7th above	CM
			Capt. W.G. Mowat M.C. rejoined from Base Depot	

D. D. & L., London, E.C.
(A10266) Wt W5300/P713 750,000 2/18 Sch. 52 Forms/C2118/16

Instructions regarding War Diaries and Intelligence Summaries are contained in F. S. Regs., Part II. and the Staff Manual respectively. Title pages will be prepared in manuscript.

WAR DIARY

or

~~INTELLIGENCE SUMMARY.~~

(*Erase heading not required.*)

Army Form C. 2118.

Place	Date	Hour	Summary of Events and Information	Remarks and references to Appendices
FRANCE 36.N.W. 36.A.NE. Batt HQ. A.23.B.1.9	9th	-	Forward guns moved to following:- C.28.a.15.20, C.22.c.30.40, C.22.c.32.45, C.22.a.80.45, I.4.d.2.1, I.4.d.3.1, I.4.a.4.4, I.3.d.7.6. Casualties 2Lt H.R. BETTINSON MC & 4 OR wounded (Gas)	ACW
	10th		Trench Routine	ACW
	11th	1130	O.O. no 65 for relief of B by D Coy on morning of 12th, C by B - night 12/13th] issued	
			Quiet day: trench routine	ACW
	12th	11.30	Relief of B Coy by D Coy complete	ACW

D. D. & L., London, E.C.
(A10266) Wt W5300/P713 750,000 2/18 Sch. 52 Forms/C2118/16

PUBLIC RECORD
OFFICE

Army Form C. 2118.

Instructions regarding War Diaries and Intelligence Summaries are contained in F. S. Regs., Part II. and the Staff Manual respectively. Title pages will be prepared in manuscript.

WAR DIARY
or
~~INTELLIGENCE SUMMARY.~~
(*Erase heading not required.*)

Place	Date	Hour	Summary of Events and Information	Remarks and references to Appendices
FRANCE Sheet 36 NW 36.A NE Batt HQ F.24.a.10.95	13		"C" Coy moved from NIEPPE area, where they staged night 12/13th, to E. outskirts of STEENWERCK; and became in Divisional Reserve. Quiet day on the whole front: indications of impending retirement on the part of the enemy	
		21.55	40th Division Order no. 218 received:- (timed 19.45) - 121st Inf. Bde to be prepared to push forward in conformity with operations to be undertaken N. of the corps front. 'B' Coy to be prepared to advance in cooperation with this brigade. The remaining Bdes. and 3 coys. of M.G. Bn. to be ready to move at 1 hours notice.	
		22.30	Order no 66 and administrative instructions in connection therewith issued: these were in conformity with 40. Div. Order no 218 (above)	QW
	14	03.00	Under orders from 121 Bde. "B". Coy moved 4 guns from reserve to come under orders of 8th R.I.R. Section HQ. established I.3.D.70.70 Remainder of day uneventful.	QW

D. D. & L., London, E.C.
(A10266) Wt W5300/P713 750,000 2/18 Sch. 52 Forms/C2118/16

PUBLIC RECORD
OFFICE

Army Form C. 2118.

WAR DIARY
or
INTELLIGENCE SUMMARY.
(Erase heading not required.)

Instructions regarding War Diaries and Intelligence Summaries are contained in F. S. Regs., Part II. and the Staff Manual respectively. Title pages will be prepared in manuscript.

Place	Date	Hour	Summary of Events and Information	Remarks and references to Appendices
FRANCE Sheet 36 NW. 36 A NE Batt H.Q. F.24. a.10.75	15	10.30	40th Division Order no. 220 timed 10.00 received: copies sent to all coys Division to push rapidly eastward: objectives J.8.b, J.3.c.4.8., D.29.d.0.7, D.22.b.0.7, QUESNOY (exclusive) Advanced guard: 121 Inf. Bde, 331 Bde RFA. "B" Coy 39 M.G. Bn. AJG	
		22.30	"B" Coy moved 2 guns to C.23.a.2.6. in touch with A Coy 8th R.I.R.	
	16	06.00	Enemy withdrew rapidly along the whole Corps front, and our advanced guard met with no resistance except at C.30. central.	
		08.00	121 Inf Bde order No 60 timed 06.00 received, giving order of march of advanced guard. GJC Reinforcements Lt C. J. Granby MC + 1 O.R	
	17	06.00	Advance continued without opposition on Corps front. Patrols reached WAMBRECHIES & Corps on right entered LILLE. GJC	
	18	10.00	Batt. H.Q. closed at F.24.a.10.75 and opened at ARMENTIERES B.30.c.9.2. 40th Div H.Q. moved to B.30.b.6.6 GJC Enemy withdrawal continued but considerable opposition was met with on the Corps front.	

D. D. & L., London, E.C.
(A10266) Wt W5300/P713 750,000 2/18 Sch. 52 Forms/C2118/16

Army Form C. 2118.

Instructions regarding War Diaries and Intelligence Summaries are contained in F. S. Regs., Part II. and the Staff Manual respectively. Title pages will be prepared in manuscript.

WAR DIARY
or
INTELLIGENCE SUMMARY.

(Erase heading not required.)

Place	Date	Hour	Summary of Events and Information	Remarks and references to Appendices
FRANCE SHEET 36 Batt H.Q. B 30c 92	18	1500	Patrols reached line LEERS - TOUFFLERS.	GJC
	19	2100	40th Div. Order No 222 timed 2000 received. Division to be relieved by flank Divisions. M.G.Bn to concentrate for rest and training at WAMBRECHIES.	GJC
Batt H.Q. E26c 81.15	20	1000	Batt H.Q. closed at B 30c 92 and opened at WAMBRECHIES at E26c 81.15. Companies rested & carried out improvements to billets. The ESCAUT was reached on the Corps front	GJC
	21	0900	Companies carried out training under Coy arrangements. No change in situation on Corps front.	GJC
	22	0900	Companies continued training. Posts were established on east bank of L'Escaut at I2a 52 & beat off two counter-attacks.	GJC
	23	0900	Training continued. Enemy continues to resist in line of L'Escaut. Reinforcements 23 O.R.	

Army Form C. 2118.

Instructions regarding War Diaries and Intelligence Summaries are contained in F. S. Regs., Part II. and the Staff Manual respectively. Title pages will be prepared in manuscript.

WAR DIARY
or
INTELLIGENCE SUMMARY.
(Erase heading not required.)

Place	Date	Hour	Summary of Events and Information	Remarks and references to Appendices
FRANCE	24	0900	Training continued	
SHEET 36		2245	40th Div Order N°224 received :- timed 2115	
Batt H.Q.			40th Div will relieve 31st Div in line on night 26/27 October	
E26c.8115			39th M.G. Bn to move to LEERS 37/G.12. on 25th Oct	
			March to be via CROIX. CROIX not to be entered before 1300	
		2315	Orders in compliance with above issued to companies.	EJC
	25	1100	Batt. moved off from WAMBRECHIES marching in order B.C.A.D. Cys	
Sheet 37		1600	Arrived LEERS. Batt. H.Q. opened at G6d42	
Batt HQ			No change in situation on Corps front	EJC
G6d42.	26	1100	"D" Coy moved off to relieve "A" Coy 31st Bn M.G.C.	
			1 Section moved into the line with positions as follows:- Section H.Q. C20a84	
			N°1 Gun C20b50, No2 gun C20c77, N°3 gun I2a42, No4 gun I2c43	
			Coy H.Q. were at NECHIN H.13.d.8.7. Remaining 3 Sections in NECHIN.	
		1800	Relief was completed without incident. Hostile artillery showed	
			some activity against PECQ and WARCOING.	
			Div. boundaries were on the N.:- GRID LINE eastwards through B13a00	
			on the S:- Southern edge of NECHIN - ESTAIMBOURG road.	
			to H.H central, thence E along line through H12 central etc.	EJC

D. D. & L., London, E.C.
(A10266) Wt W5300/P713 750,000 2/18 Sch. 52 Forms/C2118/16

Instructions regarding War Diaries and Intelligence Summaries are contained in F. S. Regs., Part II. and the Staff Manual respectively. Title pages will be prepared in manuscript.

WAR DIARY
or
INTELLIGENCE SUMMARY.
(Erase heading not required.)

Army Form C. 2118.

Place	Date	Hour	Summary of Events and Information	Remarks and references to Appendices
FRANCE SHEET 37 Batt H.Q. G6d 42	27	1145	40th Div. Order No 225 received (timed 1145) :- On night 27/28, 40th D. will extend its front Northwards. ~~[illegible]~~ N. Divisional boundary will then be as follows - E+W grid line through B13c00 & B17d1500 thence along S bank of CANAL DE L'ESPIERRE to C9d13 thence eastwards through C11d13 In accordance with above No1 Section D Coy relieved "C" Coy 14th M.G. Bn in positions at C9c3525, C9c3520, C8c4015, C8c5010, with Section HQ at C8c3020. Harassing fire was carried out on road running N+S through HERINNES Enemy artillery showed considerable activity against PECQ + WARCOING	
	28	0900	"D" Coy adjusted ~~[illegible]~~ gun positions, final dispositions being as follows:- Rt Section :- H.Q. I1d5060 No 1+2 Guns at I1d56 No3 gun I2c4080 No4 gun I2c4020 Lft Section :- H.Q. C8c3030 No5 gun C20c77, No6 gun C20b50, No7 gun C9c3520, No8 gun C9c3525 Enemy artillery continued to show some activity against the villages on our front. Reinforcements 2 O.R. [illegible signature]	

D. D. & L., London, E.C.
(A10260) Wt W5300/P713 750,000 2/18 Sch. 52 Forms/C2118/16

Instructions regarding War Diaries and Intelligence Summaries are contained in F. S. Regs., Part II. and the Staff Manual respectively. Title pages will be prepared in manuscript.

WAR DIARY
or
INTELLIGENCE SUMMARY.
(*Erase heading not required.*)

Army Form C. 2118.

Place	Date	Hour	Summary of Events and Information	Remarks and references to Appendices
FRANCE SHEET 37 Batt H.Q. G 6 d 4 2	29	1100	D Coy H.Q moved to ESTAIMBOURG H 5 c 4 2. The 2 reserve Sections were concentrated about Coy H.Q. Harassing fire was carried out on X roads I 3 a 8 9. Hostile artillery shelled WARCOING intermittently also ESTAIMBOURG - PECQ road. Reinforcements 25 O.R.s	
	30	1630	M.G's in CHATEAU at PECQ fired in support of a patrol which crossed the SHELDT and located the enemy at I 26 8030. Enemy artillery showed considerable activity, especially during afternoon and evening against WARCOING and PECQ.	CJC
	31		Enemy artillery again showed considerable activity.	
		1700	Operation Order No 68 issued:- "A" Coy to relieve "D" Coy in the line during night 31/1st & morning of 1st, relief to be complete by 6AM. Casualty 1 O.R. wounded	CJC

A. Richardson Major
Commanding 39th Army Bn. M.G. Corps.

D. D. & L., London, E.C. (A10265) Wt W5300/P713 750,000 2/15 Sch. 52 Forms/C2118/16

CONFIDENTIAL.

WAR DIARY.

of

39th (Army) Machine Gun Battalion.

From – 1st December 1918. To – 31st December. 1918.

VOLUME. 10.

Army Form C. 2118.

Instructions regarding War Diaries and Intelligence Summaries are contained in F. S. Regs., Part II. and the Staff Manual respectively. Title pages will be prepared in manuscript.

WAR DIARY
or
INTELLIGENCE SUMMARY.

(Erase heading not required.)

Place	Date	Hour	Summary of Events and Information	Remarks and references to Appendices

250

D. D. & L. London, E.C.
(A8004) Wt W1771/M2031 750,000 5/15 Sch. 52 Forms/C2118/14

Army Form C. 2118.

Instructions regarding War Diaries and Intelligence Summaries are contained in F. S. Regs., Par. II, and the Staff Manual respectively. Title pages will be prepared in manuscript.

WAR DIARY
or
~~INTELLIGENCE SUMMARY~~.
(Erase heading not required.)

Place	Date	Hour	Summary of Events and Information	Remarks and references to Appendices
FRANCE SHEET 37 Battn H.Q. G6d4,2	1	11,30	Church Parade	GB
	2		Parades under Company arrangements	
		1700	Lecture on "Flying" by Captain P. BEWSHER DSO, RAF	GB
	3		Parades under company arrangements	GB
	4		Parades under Company arrangements	GB

A6945 Wt. W11422/M1160 350,000 12/16 D. D. & L. Forms/C./2118/14.

Army Form C. 2118.

WAR DIARY
or
~~INTELLIGENCE SUMMARY.~~
(Erase heading not required.)

Instructions regarding War Diaries and Intelligence Summaries are contained in F. S. Regs., Part II. and the Staff Manual respectively. Title pages will be prepared in manuscript.

Place	Date	Hour	Summary of Events and Information	Remarks and references to Appendices
	5		Parades under Company arrangements	[illegible]
	6		Parades under company arrangements	
			Re-inforcement of 10 other ranks received	[illegible]
	7		Parades under company arrangements	
			The following Honours and Awards were notified in [illegible] D.R.O.	
			Major R.W. FYFFE - Croix de Guerre (Palm with gold star)	
			5356 Sergeant J HILL - (Bronze with silver star)	
			11237 Sergeant O'DONNELL -	[illegible]
			35374 Pte F STENNING - (Bronze with bronze star)	
		14.00	His Majesty the King passed along road TOURNAI - TEMPLEUVE -	
			ROUBAIX and the Battalion lined the route at TEMPLEUVE	

A6945 Wt. W11422/M1160 350,000 12/16 D. D. & L. Forms/C./2118/14.

Army Form C. 2118.

Instructions regarding War Diaries and Intelligence Summaries are contained in F. S. Regs., Part II. and the Staff Manual respectively. Title pages will be prepared in manuscript.

WAR DIARY
or
~~INTELLIGENCE SUMMARY.~~
(Erase heading not required.)

Place	Date	Hour	Summary of Events and Information	Remarks and references to Appendices
	8	11.00	Church Parade	
		15.00	The Battalion sent a detachment – strength 200 all ranks – to a presentation of decorations by the Divisional Commander in the square at LANNOY	GB
			Re-inforcement of 1 other rank received	
	9		Parades under company arrangements	GB
	10	09.15	The Battalion paraded on green E of CHURCH, LEERS and proceeded to NECHIN for practice Divisional Ceremonial Parade	GB
			Demobilization of Industrial Group 3 commenced.	
	11	09.15	Battalion parade for practice of Ceremonial Drill.	GB

A6945 Wt. W11422/M1160 350,000 12/16 D. D. & L. Forms/C./2118/14.

Instructions regarding War Diaries and Intelligence Summaries are contained in F. S. Regs., Par. II, and the Staff Manual respectively. Title pages will be prepared in manuscript.

WAR DIARY
or
~~INTELLIGENCE SUMMARY.~~
(Erase heading not required.)

Army Form C. 2118.

Place	Date	Hour	Summary of Events and Information	Remarks and references to Appendices
	12		Parades under company arrangements	AB
	13		Parades under company arrangements	AB
	14		Parades under company arrangements Re-inforcement of 1 other rank received	AB
	15	11.10	Church Parade The Battalion sent a detachment of 12 officers 1200 ORs to a special Inter-denominational service held at ROUBAIX	AB
	16		Parades under company arrangements Re-inforcement of 3 other ranks received	AB

Instructions regarding War Diaries and Intelligence Summaries are contained in F. S. Regs., Part II. and the Staff Manual respectively. Title pages will be prepared in manuscript.

WAR DIARY
or
~~INTELLIGENCE SUMMARY.~~
(Erase heading not required.)

Army Form C. 2118.

Place	Date	Hour	Summary of Events and Information	Remarks and references to Appendices
	17	09.15	The Battalion paraded on the Green by the Church LEERS. It proceeded to NECHIN, taking up a position on the right flank of the 40 Division, and was reviewed by LIEUT-GENERAL Sir BEAUVOIR de LISLE KCB, DSO., Commanding XV Corps	GB
	18		Parades under company arrangements	GB
	19		Parades under company arrangements	GB
	20		Parades under company arrangements	GB
	21		Re-inforcement of 10 other ranks received	
	21		Parades under company arrangements	GB

D. D. & L., London, E.C.
(A5001) Wt. W1-71/M2031 750,000 5/17 Sch. 52 Forms/C2118/14

Army Form C. 2118.

Instructions regarding War Diaries and Intelligence Summaries are contained in F. S. Regs., Part II. and the Staff Manual respectively. Title pages will be prepared in manuscript.

WAR DIARY
or
~~INTELLIGENCE SUMMARY.~~

(Erase heading not required.)

Place	Date	Hour	Summary of Events and Information	Remarks and references to Appendices
	22	09.30	Church Parade	GB
	23		Parades under company arrangements. A detachment of 2 officers & 122 ORs visited LILLE by divisional arrangement Re-inforcement of 1 officer and 9 other ranks received	GB
	24		Parades under company arrangements	GB
	25	11.30	Church parade	GB
	26		Observed, as far as possible, as a general holiday.	GB
	27		Parades under company arrangements Re-inforcement of 4 other ranks received	GB

D. D. & L., London, E.C.
(A8001) Wt. W1 71/M2031 750,000 5/17 Sch. 52 Forms/C2118/14

256

Instructions regarding War Diaries and Intelligence Summaries are contained in F. S. Regs., Part II. and the Staff Manual respectively. Title pages will be prepared in manuscript.

WAR DIARY
or
INTELLIGENCE SUMMARY.
(*Erase heading not required.*)

Army Form C. 2118.

Place	Date	Hour	Summary of Events and Information	Remarks and references to Appendices
	28		Parades under company arrangements	GB
	29	0930	Church parade	GB
	30		Parades under company arrangements	GB
	31		Parades under company arrangements	GB

A Fleetwood Wilson Lt Col
Comdg 39th (Army) Bn M.G.C.

D. D. & L., London, E.C.
(A8004) Wt. W1771/M2031 750,000 5/17 Sch. 52 Forms/C2118/14

7

V8/11

Confidential.

War Diary

of

39th (Army) Machine Gun Battalion.

From 1st January 1919. To January 31st 1919.

Volume 11

Instructions regarding War Diaries and Intelligence Summaries are contained in F. S. Regs., Part II. and the Staff Manual respectively. Title pages will be prepared in manuscript.

WAR DIARY

or

~~INTELLIGENCE~~ SUMMARY.

(Erase heading not required.)

Army Form C. 2118.

Place	Date	Hour	Summary of Events and Information	Remarks and references to Appendices

258

A6945 Wt. W11422/M1160 350,000 12/16 D. D. & L. Forms/C./2118/14.

Army Form C. 2118.

Instructions regarding War Diaries and Intelligence Summaries are contained in F. S. Regs., Part II. and the Staff Manual respectively. Title pages will be prepared in manuscript.

WAR DIARY
or
~~INTELLIGENCE SUMMARY~~.
(Erase heading not required.)

Place	Date	Hour	Summary of Events and Information	Remarks and references to Appendices
FRANCE	1919 Aug. 1.		Company Training 1 O.R. demobilized	JJB.
Sheet 37	2.		Company Training	JJB
Batt.	3.		Company Training. Educational classes resumed.	JJB.
M.G.C. 6d42	4.		Parades under Company arrangements.	JJB.
	5.	9.30	Church Parade C of E. 2 O.Rs demobilized	JJB
	6.		Under Company Arrangements. 7 " "	JJB
	7.		Parades under Company arrangements. 1 O.R. demobilized	JJB
	8.		Parades under Company arrangements. 6 O.Rs "	JJB.
	9.		Parades under Company arrangements. Hon Lt + QM Thomas + 3 ORs demobilized	JJB.
	10.		Parades under Company arrangements. 1	JJB
			Following decorations were notified in D.R.O. 10. ORs joined unit	
			Belgian Croix de Guerre Lt Col. A. Fleetwood Wilson	
			do. 65802 Sgt. H. R. Smith.	
			do. 84179. Signaller P. E. Morgan.	
	11.		Parades under Company arrangements. 1 O.R rejoined unit	JJB.
			Reinforcements of 9 other ranks arrived 9. O.Rs demobilized	JJB.

Army Form C. 2118.

Instructions regarding War Diaries and Intelligence Summaries are contained in F. S. Regs., Part II, and the Staff Manual respectively. Title pages will be prepared in manuscript.

WAR DIARY
or
~~INTELLIGENCE~~ ~~SUMMARY~~.
(Erase heading not required.)

Place	Date	Hour	Summary of Events and Information	Remarks and references to Appendices
FRANCE	12.	11.30.	Nonconformist Church parade 4 O.Rs demobilized	JJB.
SHEET 37	13.		Company Training 9 O.Rs "	JJB
Battn.	14.		Company Training	JJB
MGC 6d 42	15.		Company Training B. C + D Coy. A Coy paraded drill order for inspection by the Commanding Officer.	JJB
	16.		Company Training A. C + D Coy. B Company paraded drill order for inspection by the commanding Officer.	JJB
	17.		Company Training A B + D Coy. C Coy paraded drill order for inspection by the Commanding Officer.	JJB
	18.		Colonel C. C. Hewitt D.S.O. M.C. 5th Army M.G.O. inspected armouries and awarded prizes as follows 1. D Coy 3 Section 2. C. Coy 3 Section. + 3 A Coy 3 Section. 11 O.Rs demobilized	JJB
	19.	9.30.	Church parade C of E. 13 O'Rs demobilized	JJB
	20.		Company Training 25 O.R's "	JJB
			Reinforcements of 2 other ranks. Lts Dare, Wright + 2nd Lts Pickles, Nicholls Hodgson	
	21.		Company Training + 21 O'Rs demobilized.	JJB

A6945 Wt. W11422/M1160 35,000 12/16 D. D. & L. Forms/C./2118/14.

Instructions regarding War Diaries and Intelligence Summaries are contained in F. S. Regs., Par. II. and the Staff Manual respectively. Title pages will be prepared in manuscript.

WAR DIARY
or
~~INTELLIGENCE~~ ~~SUMMARY~~.
(Erase heading not required.)

Army Form C. 2118.

Place	Date	Hour	Summary of Events and Information	Remarks and references to Appendices
FRANCE	22.		Company Training 2nd Lt. E.R. Pike. demobilized	J.J.B.
SHEET 34	23		Company Training.	J.J.B
Battn	24.		Company Training	J.J.B.
M.G.C. 6 d 42	25.		Company Training Lt. H.H. Sturt + 2 O.Rs demobilized	J.J.B.
	26	9.15	Church Parade C. of E. Major H.K. Royle + 16 O.Rs demobilized	J.J.B.
		11.30	do Presbyterians + Nonconformists. ~~Lt~~	
	27.		Parades under Company Arrangements. Lts. Ister, Blaw + 2nd Lt Corrall + 25 O.Rs demob	J.J.B.
	28.		Parades under Company Arrangements. Major Platts, Lts Booth, Dolley, Graham + Janson + 350 R demob	
	29.		Parades under Company Arrangements. Capt. Higginbottom + 2nd Lts Perkins J. Richardson, Guthrie, Lalkin. + 43 O.Rs. demobilized.	J.J.B.
	30.		Parades under Company Arrangements.	J.J.B.
	31.		Parades under Company Arrangements.	J.J.B.

[signature] Lt. Col
Commanding 39th (Army) Battalion
Machine Gun Corps

A6945 Wt. W11422/M1160 350,000 12/16 D. D. & L. Forms/C./2118/14.

V8 12

57

Confidential.

War Diary
of
39th (Army) Machine Gun Battalion

From 1st February 1919.

To 28th February 1919.

Volume 12.

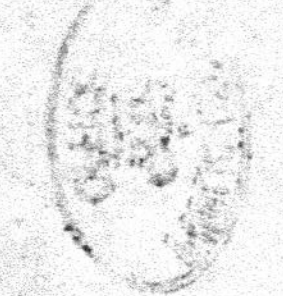

Army Form C. 2118.

Instructions regarding War Diaries and Intelligence Summaries are contained in F. S. Regs., Part II. and the Staff Manual respectively. Title pages will be prepared in manuscript.

WAR DIARY
or
INTELLIGENCE SUMMARY.

(*Erase heading not required.*)

Place	Date	Hour	Summary of Events and Information	Remarks and references to Appendices

D. D. & L., London, E.C.
(A8:04) Wt W1771/M2031 750,000 5/ Sch. 52 Forms/C2118/14

Army Form C. 2118.

WAR DIARY
or
INTELLIGENCE SUMMARY.
(Erase heading not required.)

Instructions regarding War Diaries and Intelligence Summaries are contained in F. S. Regs., Part II. and the Staff Manual respectively. Title pages will be prepared in manuscript.

Place	Date 1919 Feb	Hour	Summary of Events and Information	Remarks and references to Appendices
FRANCE	1		Parades under Company Arrangements.	
Sheet 37			6 other ranks left for demobilization.	EJC
Battn	2	9.30	Church parade Church of England	
M.G.			6 other ranks left for demobilization	EJC
G.b.d.4.2	3.		Parades under Company arrangements.	
			Lieut H.T. Egerton 2nd Lieut S.L. Tarvis + 9 other ranks left for demobilization	EJC
	4		Parades under Company arrangements.	EJC
	5	10.00	Medical Inspection Parades under Company arrangements.	
		13.30	Lecture by Captain + Adjutant E.J. Mills O.B.E. on the Army of Occupation	EJC
	6		Parades under Company Arrangements.	
			18 other ranks left for demobilization	EJC
	7		Parades under Company Arrangements	EJC
			26 other ranks left for demobilization.	
	8		Parades under Company arrangements.	
			18 other ranks left for demobilization	EJC

D. D. & L., London, E.C.
(A10266) Wt W5300/P713 750,000 2/18 Sch. 52 Forms/C2118/16

Army Form C. 2118.

WAR DIARY
or
INTELLIGENCE SUMMARY.
(Erase heading not required.)

Instructions regarding War Diaries and Intelligence Summaries are contained in F. S. Regs., Part II. and the Staff Manual respectively. Title pages will be prepared in manuscript.

Place	Date	Hour	Summary of Events and Information	Remarks and references to Appendices
		~~10.45~~	~~Church parade Church of England~~	
	9	18.00	Voluntary Service	
			47 other ranks left for demobilization	EJC
	10		Bathing Parade	EJC
	11		Parades under Company arrangement	EJC
	12	10.00	Medical Inspection Parades under Company arrangement	EJC
	13		Parades under Company arrangement	EJC
			2nd Lt H. K. Ford left for demobilization	
	14		Parades under Company arrangement	EJC
	15		Parades under Company arrangement	EJC
	16	10.00	Holy Communion Voluntary	EJC
		18.00	Voluntary service	
	17		Parades under Company arrangement	
			Major L. W. Evans M.C. left for duty at 3rd London General Hospital	EJC
	18		Bathing Parade	EJC
	19	10.00	Medical Inspection	EJC
	20		Parades under Company arrangement	EJC

D. D. & L., London, E.C.
(A10266) Wt W5300/P713 750,000 2/18 Sch. 52 Forms/C2118/16

Army Form C. 2118.

Instructions regarding War Diaries and Intelligence Summaries are contained in F. S. Regs., Part II. and the Staff Manual respectively. Title pages will be prepared in manuscript.

WAR DIARY
or
INTELLIGENCE SUMMARY.
(*Erase heading not required.*)

Place	Date	Hour	Summary of Events and Information	Remarks and references to Appendices
	21		Parades under Company Arrangement.	[illegible]
	22	9.30	Route March Drill Order	[illegible]
	23	10.00	Holy Communion Voluntary	
		18.00	Voluntary Service	[illegible]
	24		Parades under Company Arrangements	[illegible]
	25		Parades under Company Arrangements.	[illegible]
	26	10.00	Medical Inspection. Parades under Company arrangements.	[illegible]
	27		Bathing Parades	[illegible]
	28		Parades under Company arrangements.	[illegible]

A. Richardson
Major
28/2/19. Comdg 39th (Army) Bn Machine Gun Corps

D. D. & L., London, E.C. (A8001) Wt. W1771/M2031 750,000 5/17 Sch. 52 Forms/C2118/14

PUBLIC RECORD
OFFICE

21

39

VR 13

Ceased

Confidential.

War Diary of 39th (Army) Machine Gun Battalion

From 1st March 1919 To 19th March 1919

Army Form C. 2118.

Instructions regarding War Diaries and Intelligence Summaries are contained in F. S. Regs., Par. II, and the Staff Manual respectively. Title pages will be prepared in manuscript.

WAR DIARY
or
INTELLIGENCE SUMMARY.

(*Erase heading not required.*)

Place	Date	Hour	Summary of Events and Information	Remarks and references to Appendices

266

A6945 Wt. W11422/M1160 350,000 12/16 D. D. & L. Forms/C./2118/14.

Army Form C. 2118.

Instructions regarding War Diaries and Intelligence Summaries are contained in F. S. Regs., Part II. and the Staff Manual respectively. Title pages will be prepared in manuscript.

WAR DIARY
or
INTELLIGENCE SUMMARY.
(Erase heading not required.)

Place	Date	Hour	Summary of Events and Information	Remarks and references to Appendices
FRANCE	1		Parades under Company arrangements	
SHEET	2	10.00	Holy Communion	
37G	3		Company arrangements.	
[illegible]	4		Company arrangements.	
M G	5	10.00	Medical Inspection	
Battn			Company arrangements	
	6		Bathing Parades	
	7		Company arrangements	
	8		Company arrangements.	
	9		40 Other ranks to [illegible] Battalion for demobilization	
	10		Company arrangements.	
	11		Company arrangements	
	12	11.00	Medical Inspection Parade Company arrangements	
			Captain E J Mills O.B.E. Adjutant [illegible] Battalion [illegible] 3rd London General Hospital	
	13		Bathing Parade	

D. D. & L., London, E.C.
(A8001) Wt. W1 71/M2031 750,000 5/17 Sch. 52 Forms/C2118/14

Instructions regarding War Diaries and Intelligence Summaries are contained in F. S. Regs., Part II. and the Staff Manual respectively. Title pages will be prepared in manuscript.

WAR DIARY
or
INTELLIGENCE SUMMARY.
(Erase heading not required.)

Army Form C. 2118.

Place	Date	Hour	Summary of Events and Information	Remarks and references to Appendices
	14		Company arrangements	
			[illegible] O. R. transferred to 3rd [illegible]	
	15		Company arrangements	
	16	10 00	Church of England Service (Voluntary) [illegible]	
		11 00	Holy Communion (Voluntary).	
		18 00	Evening Service (Voluntary).	
SHEET.	17	10 00	Battalion [illegible] for [illegible] to [illegible]	
3E/L		14 00	Divisional Commander's inspection and farewell [illegible]	
Q.7.b.4	18		Company arrangements	
	19	[illegible]	[illegible] of Battalion entrained [illegible] to [illegible]	

D. D. & L., London, E.C.
(A8104) Wt W1771/M2031 750,000 5/19 Sch. 52 Forms/C2118/14

33RD DIVISION
99TH INFY BDE

BDE HEADQUARTERS
17TH BN ROY. FUS.
22ND .. .. ..
23RD .. .. ..
24TH .. .. ..

NOV 1915.

2 DIV

PUBLIC RECORD
OFFICE

www.ingramcontent.com/pod-product-compliance
Lightning Source LLC
Chambersburg PA
CBHW081538160426
43191CB00011B/1786
* 9 7 8 1 4 7 4 5 1 9 0 7 6 *